How to use Explore

Issue 107

The 92 daily readings in this issue of Explore are designed to help you understand and apply the Bible as you read it each day.

It's serious!

We suggest that you allow 15 minutes each day to work through the Bible passage with the notes. It should be a meal, not a snack! Readings from other parts of the Bible can throw valuable light on the study passage. These cross-references can be skipped if you are already feeling full up, but will expand your grasp of the Bible. Explore uses the NIV2011 Bible translation, but you can also use it with the NIV1984 or ESV translations.

Sometimes a prayer box will encourage you to stop and pray through the lessons—but it is always important to allow time to pray for God's Spirit to bring his word to life, and to shape the way we think and live through it.

We're serious!

All of us who work on Explore share a passion for getting the Bible into people's lives. We fiercely hold to the Bible as God's word—to honour and follow, not to explain away.

1 Find a time you can read the Bible each day

2 Find a place where you can be quiet and think

3 Ask God to help you understand

4 Carefully read through the Bible passage for today

5 Study the verses with *Explore*, taking time to think

6 Pray about what you have read

the good book
COMPANY

BIBLICAL | RELEVANT | ACCESSIBLE

Welcome to *explore*

Being a Christian isn't a skill you learn, nor is it a lifestyle choice. It's about having a real relationship with the living God through his Son, Jesus Christ. The Bible tells us that this relationship is like a marriage.

It's important to start with this, because it is easy to view the practice of daily Bible reading as a Christian duty, or a hard discipline that is just one more thing to get done in our busy lives.

But the Bible is God speaking to us: opening his mind to us on how he thinks, what he wants for us and what his plans are for the world. And most importantly, it tells us what he has done for us in sending his Son, Jesus Christ, into the world. It's the way that the Spirit shows Jesus to us, and changes us as we behold his glory.

Here are a few suggestions for making your time with God more of a joy than a burden:

- *Time:* Find a time when you will not be disturbed. Many people have found that the morning is the best time as it sets you up for the day. But whatever works for you is right for you.

- *Place:* Jesus says that we are not to make a great show of our religion *(see Matthew 6:5-6)*, but rather, to pray with the door to our room shut. Some people plan to get to work a few minutes earlier and get their Bible out in an office or some other quiet corner.

- *Prayer:* Although *Explore* helps with specific prayer ideas from the passage, do try to develop your own lists to pray through. Use the flap inside the back cover to help with this. And allow what you read in the Scriptures to shape what you pray for yourself, the world and others.

- *Feast:* You can use the "Bible in a year" line at the bottom of each page to help guide you through the entire Scriptures throughout 2024. This year, the passages each day are linked, showing how God makes and keeps his promises. We're grateful to Katherine Fedor of treasureinthebible.com for her permission to use this Bible-reading plan. You'll find passages to read six days a week—Sunday is a "day off", or a day to catch up!

- *Share:* As the saying goes, *expression deepens impression.* So try to cultivate the habit of sharing with others what you have learned. Why not join our Facebook group to share your encouragements, questions and prayer requests? Search for *Explore: For your daily walk with God.*

And enjoy it! As you read God's word and God's Spirit works in your mind and your heart, you are going to see Jesus, and appreciate more of his love for you and his promises to you. That's amazing!

Carl Laferton is the Editorial Director of The Good Book Company

ROMANS: Who and what?

The letter of Romans is all about the gospel: what it is, why we need it and what difference it makes. The gospel dominates, from the very first verse.

The writer

Read Romans 1:1-7

❷ *Who is the letter from (v 1)? To (v 7)?*

❷ *What is Paul's job, and passion (v 1, 5)?*

To be "set apart" is to be separated from other things, to pursue only one thing. The gospel is so great that Paul is willing to separate himself from anything in order to live for it and share it.

The message

❷ *What do we learn about...*
  • *where we find the gospel (v 2)?*
  • *who the gospel is about (v 3-4)?*
  • *what the gospel produces (v 5)?*

Paul wants people to obey God—but the obedience he wants is one that springs from faith. What that means is one of the main themes of the letter; but, in short, it is an obedient heart and life that comes from knowing that we are accepted and righteous in God's eyes through our faith in his Son, Jesus Christ.

⌄ Apply

The Christian life is not about obeying God to be accepted. Nor is it about being accepted and therefore not obeying him. It is about "the obedience that comes from faith".

❷ *Do you ever obey because you think you have to, to stay forgiven?*

❷ *Do you ever disobey because you know you don't **have** to obey?*

❷ *How do you think faith in the Lord Jesus motivates us to want to obey?*

The visit

Read Romans 1:8-15

❷ *What is Paul's attitude to the Roman Christians (v 8-10a)?*

❷ *What is striking about this, given that Paul has never met them?*

❷ *Why does Paul "long to see" this church (v 11-13)?*

Paul, the great apostle, does not say in verse 12 "so that you may be encouraged by me". Rather, he says so that "you and I may be mutually encouraged by each other's faith".

❷ *What does this tell us about what all Christians need?*

Notice Paul wants to preach the gospel (v 15) to the church in Rome, i.e. to Christians.

❷ *What does this tell us about what all Christians need?*

⌄ Apply

❷ *This week, how can you...*
  • *allow others' faith to encourage yours?*
  • *use your abilities to encourage other Christians?*
  • *make sure you are reflecting on the gospel message?*

Bible in a year: 1 Kings 1 – 2 • Psalm 94, Psalm 112, Psalm 139

Eager or ashamed?

There are two ways to feel about sharing the gospel: eager (v 15), or ashamed (v 16). In these two verses, Paul will help us to be "not ashamed of the gospel".

TIME OUT

❓ *Why is the gospel shameful, or offensive, to people?*

Here are four reasons. The gospel says...
- salvation is undeserved; it offends moral people who think their goodness means they don't need saving.

- we are all sinners; it offends the popular belief in the innate goodness of humanity.

- only Jesus can save; it offends those who think that all spiritual paths lead to the same place.

- the road to glory is one of suffering and sacrifice; it offends those who want following Jesus to be easy and comfortable.

Read Romans 1:16-17

I am *not* ashamed

❓ *Why is Paul not ashamed of the gospel (v 16)?*

❓ *What does it do (v 16)? Who for?*

This power goes to work in anyone and everyone who "believes". Here we have the first explicit statement in Romans that the only way to receive the gospel and its saving power is through faith. Notice that the gospel does not come with power; it *is* power. It is the power of God in verbal form, and it has the power to change, transform, and give life to people. It does what no other power on earth can do; it saves us.

🔽 Apply

❓ *Do you ever doubt or forget the power of the gospel? What causes this?*

❓ *What difference would it make to you if you had a real grasp on how powerful the gospel is?*

What the gospel is

❓ *What is "revealed" in the gospel (v 17)?*

This is a positional word; it means to be in right standing with someone, to not owe them anything. It means to be completely acceptable to someone. So verse 17 is saying that right standing from God can be received from God (chapter 3 will show us how this is possible).

❓ *So why is this gospel about far more than simply "being forgiven"?*

The gospel is a complete reversal of both the natural tendency of the human heart and the universal thrust of other religions. Everyone else thinks of salvation as being about providing our own righteousness to offer to God. The gospel says salvation is all about receiving a righteousness from God.

⌃ Pray

Thank God for this wonderful gospel. Ask God to make you so excited about what the gospel is, and does, that you are eager about living for it and sharing it.

Why we need saving

Verse 18 literally begins with the word "For" (ESV). The next chapters will answer the questions: Why do I need saving? Why do I need to receive righteousness from God?

God's wrath

Read Romans 1:18-20

❓ *What does verse 18 tell us about God's "wrath", his settled anger?*

❓ *Why are all people "without excuse" (v 19-20)?*

All of Paul's confidence, joy and passion for the gospel rests on the assumption that all humans are, apart from the gospel, under God's wrath. If you don't understand or believe in the wrath of God, the gospel will not thrill, empower, or move you.

Human worship

Read Romans 1:21-25

❓ *What do all people do instead of recognising God as God, and living in gratitude to him (v 21-23)?*

This is counterfeit-god construction. We were created to worship God; so, if we reject him, we will worship something else. Something must give our life purpose and meaning; and we serve that "something". We will either worship the Creator or something he has created. And no created thing can satisfy us (because they're not God); and so we find ourselves enslaved by them.

⌄ Apply

Think of an idol you find it easy to worship, serve and obey instead of God.

❓ *Why is that thing attractive to you?*

❓ *Can you identify how it fails to deliver what it promises, and enslaves instead?*

Read Romans 1:26-32

Verses 26-27 are the longest passage in the Bible specifically about homosexuality. Here, homosexuality is described as "against nature" (*para phusin*). This means it is a violation of the nature God gave us; a sin. But notice that it comes after Paul has identified the root of all sin: worshipping something other than God. And it comes before a long list of other sins, including envy and gossiping. Active homosexuality is no more or less sinful than these—all come from worshipping the created, rather than the Creator.

❓ *Do any of the outworkings of "a depraved mind" in verses 29-31 particularly surprise or challenge you?*

This whole section is about God's present wrath, which is being revealed (v 18). In other words, God's wrath is simply to "give us over" to the things we worship and want—yet which cannot satisfy or save us.

⌃ Pray

Use this passage to confess to God ways in which you worship created things.
Then use it to prompt you to praise God for who he is, and thank him for his gospel.

The religious problem

Some people—religious, good people—would read Romans 1 and say, "Yes, of course God's wrath lies on the immoral. But we're not like that."

Self-judgment

Read Romans 2:1-11

❷ *What does Paul say about people who "pass judgment" on someone else (that is, accept that others deserve God's wrath, but don't think that they themselves do)?*

The 20th-century theologian Francis Schaeffer called these verses "the invisible tape recorder". It is as though there is a tape recorder around our necks, recording what we say about how others ought to live. At the last day, God will play the tape, judge us on the basis of what our own words say are the standards for human behaviour, and no one in history will be able to escape being condemned by their own words.

❷ *How is someone who thinks they don't deserve judgment actually misunderstanding what God is doing (v 4)?*

❷ *What is this person doing (v 5)?*

❷ *Why is verse 6 surprising?*

Paul is not contradicting 1:17, where he said that we must receive righteousness, because we cannot "do" enough to become righteous ourselves. His point here is that on the day of judgment good works are the evidence of our salvation, not the basis of it. Just as the apples on an apple tree prove it's alive, but don't provide life, so the good works we do prove that our faith in Christ has made us alive.

❷ *What does Paul add about God's judgment in 2:11?*

Conscience-judgment

Read Romans 2:12-16

This paragraph is complex! The basic argument is: we are judged by God's law only if we have it (v 12-13); but those without the law sometimes know what is right, and therefore do it (v 14)—showing that the law is intuitively known (v 15). So when someone who hasn't been taught God's law knows what is right, yet doesn't do it, their own thoughts accuse them—they are deserving of judgment.

Chapter 2 is all about Paul showing the Jews (and all religious people) that they have missed the whole point of the gospel. By relying on their own righteousness, they are running from salvation just as much as irreligious people, who rely on satisfying their appetites (1:18-32).

☑ Apply

Paul's challenge is: if you do not feel like a hopeless sinner, whom God would have a perfect right to reject this minute because of the state of your life, you are denying the gospel.

❷ *How does this challenge you?*

Call yourself a Christian?

Remember, in this whole chapter Paul is addressing the religious person, who thought, "I am not like the pagan. I am moral and religious, so I am not under God's judgment."

Relying on goodness?

Read Romans 2:17-24

> ❷ *What were the Jews of Paul's day proud of (v 17-20—I count six things)?*

All this boils down, basically, to a pride in their moral decency and virtue.

> ❷ *What is the challenge to them at the beginning of verse 21?*

Paul asks them to consider three ways they may not be practising what they preach (v 21-23). The third is striking, because there is no record of Jews taking idol-statues from pagan temples. So this is likely figurative; Paul is saying that underneath their outward religiosity, the Jews are worshipping idols just as much as those who go to idol-temples. They may "abhor idols" outwardly, but if inwardly they find meaning in power, comfort, possessions, sex, etc. then they are idolaters.

> ❷ *What is the tragic result of this kind of hypocritical religion (v 24)?*

Relying on ceremony?

Read Romans 2:25-29

Circumcision was the religious ceremony in which a Jew was brought into the community of Israel.

> ❷ *How much does circumcision matter, does Paul say (v 25-27)?*

> ❷ *What "circumcision" matters (v 29)?*

No religious ceremony or observance can change the heart. Only the Holy Spirit can do this, and he isn't limited by whether or not someone is circumcised or baptised, etc.

···· TIME OUT ·······································

Insert "Christian" for "Jew", and "baptism" or "church membership" for "circumcision", and then paraphrase v 17-20 and 25-29.

✅ Apply

Just because we call ourselves Christians, doesn't mean we have living faith. How can we tell if our faith is empty and we are facing judgment (even if we're an active church member)? Paul alludes to four signs:

1. A theoretical-only approach to the Bible (v 21). We don't allow ourselves to be challenged and changed by it.

2. A feeling of moral superiority (v 17). We look down on others, and are defensive when our weaknesses are exposed.

3. Lack of inner spiritual life (v 29). We don't pray, or know God loves us.

4. Hypocrisy (v 22).

> ❷ *Do any of these particularly challenge you?*

Re-read verse 29 and ask God's Spirit to work in your heart, increasing—or giving—living faith.

Bible in a year: Psalm 45 • Matthew 25 • Luke 14 • Revelation 19 ⬇

Every mouth silenced

Paul now reaches his conclusion. Everyone needs saving—needs to receive God's righteousness—because "there is no one righteous, not even one" (v 10).

Q+A

Read Romans 3:1-8

❓ *What is good about being Jewish (v 2)?*

The questions of verses 3-8 may not be ones we would naturally think of as we read chapters 1 – 2—they're the objections of 1st-century Jews. But the fact Paul deals with them shows that he was a man who took time to think about the worldview of those he was speaking to, and who made the effort to deal with objections to the gospel.

No one

Read Romans 3:9-18

❓ *What is true of everyone—Jew and Gentile, religious and unreligious (v 9)?*

This is not to say that everyone is equally sinful. But all are equally condemned, because neither the religious person nor the unreligious person has a righteous heart.

❓ *In verses 11-18, how does sin affect our...*
- *minds?*
- *motives?*
- *will?*
- *tongues?*
- *relationships?*
- *attitude towards God?*

How can it be true that "no one ... does good" (v 12)? Because the motive matters. If you help an elderly lady across the road (a good act) because you hope she'll give you money (a bad motive), you are not doing good! And if we do good deeds in order to be saved, we are doing good for ourselves,

and not for God. It is all selfishly motivated. Good deeds are not done for God—and thus are not truly good—unless a person has accepted and grasped the gospel. But once we know we are loved by God because of Christ, then we are freed to "do good"—to feed the hungry, visit the sick, clothe the poor, and all for their sake and God's sake.

✅ Apply

❓ *How does this idea of "doing good" both challenge you and motivate you?*

Silence

Read Romans 3:19-20

❓ *Why will "every mouth ... be silenced" (v 19) when judgment comes?*

❓ *What can the law not do? What can it do (v 20)?*

A silent mouth is a spiritual condition—the attitude which knows that we cannot save ourselves, has no defence to make, and no goodness to offer. Without a silent mouth, we will never come to God with empty hands to receive the righteousness he offers.

✅ Apply

❓ *Do you, deep down, think that when you stand before God in judgment, you will have something to say? Have you attained the spiritual condition of a silent mouth?*

Exaltation and destruction

It often feels as if God's kingdom is in retreat, overwhelmed by the forces of secularism and other religions. Is that right? Is Jesus overwhelmed by the forces that oppose him?

The King's exaltation

Read Psalm 21:1-7

- ❓ *What has the Lord given the king of God's people (v 1-6)?*
- ❓ *Why has he given him these things (v 7)?*

Read Philippians 2:5-11

- ❓ *How has Jesus reflected the attitude of the king in Psalm 21?*
- ❓ *How has the Lord responded to him, in keeping with the pattern set in the psalm?*

⬇ Apply

When reading any part of the Bible, it's always really important for us to ask ourselves, "Who is this really about?" Often, our instinct will be to assume that it is all about us! But these kingly psalms of David are about God's King before they are ever about us. And so, ultimately, they point to King Jesus and speak of him. Once we have that clear, there are often practical personal lessons for us to learn. Here in Psalm 21, the king sets a model (which Jesus fulfilled perfectly) for us to follow.

The psalm reminds us that King Jesus rejoices in the Lord's strength (v 1) and trusts unshakeably in the "love of the Most High" (v 7).

- ❓ *Is that the attitude of your own heart today? How/how not?*

Pray that it might be. After all, King Jesus proved by his resurrection and ascension that the Lord can be trusted!

The King's victory

Read Psalm 21:8-13

The Lord is clearly angry here.

- ❓ *Why is he so angry?*
- ❓ *How and where do you see verse 11 happening today?*
- ❓ *What will happen to the king's enemies? (Notice the very sobering pictures used here.) When will all this take place?*

⬆ Pray

Using the words of verse 12 to get yourself started, praise and thank God for the sure victory of Jesus over his enemies.

Think of people you know who have not bowed the knee to King Jesus and who stand opposed to him. Ask the Lord to have mercy on them, turning their hearts from rebellion to repentance before it is too late.

⬇

Righteousness revealed

For two chapters, Paul has been underlining the terrible truth that every human is under judgment. None of us is right with God. "But now…"

Righteousness

Read Romans 3:21-26

Righteousness is the crucial word in this passage; and the word "justified" is, in the Greek, the same word. Righteousness is a legal standing of acceptability which is the result of perfect behaviour (e.g. to be "right with the law" is to have completely obeyed it, so that it cannot charge you).

> ❷ *What do verses 21-23 tell us about being right with God?*
> • *Where it comes from.*
> • *Where it doesn't come from.*
> • *How it comes to us.*
> • *Why we need it.*

The just justifier

But why does righteousness only come through faith in Christ Jesus (v 22); through faith in his blood, his death (v 25)? Why can't God just forgive people?

The two vital words are "redemption" (v 24—which means to free someone by paying a price), and "sacrifice of atonement", literally "propitiation" (v 25—which means the turning away of someone's anger).

> ❷ *So what did Jesus' death achieve (v 24)?*
> ❷ *How (v 25)?*
> ❷ *What does the cross demonstrate (v 26)?*

> ❷ *How does Paul clarify what he means by this in the rest of verse 26?*

This is the wonder of the cross. In the very same stroke it satisfied both the love of God (that wanted to save people) and the justice of God (that demands punishment of sin). God is just—humanity is punished for sin; and God is able to justify (i.e. make righteous) sinners; the perfect man Jesus was punished in our place.

On the cross, God's wrath and love, his justice and justifying, are both demonstrated, expressed and vindicated completely.

If our view of God is as a God of love who does not insist on standards and does not punish wrongdoing, then God becomes uncaring and indifferent (as well as non-existent). We are spiritual orphans. But, on the other hand, a wrathful God without grace makes us feel crushed and despairing, or angry and defiant, never able to live up to his standards.

At the cross, we find that God is a God of wrath and grace. He is a Father worth having, and a Father we can have.

Pray

Spend some time reading through the verses, using each phrase to meditate on what happened at the cross, and praising God for it.

Two applications

Paul has presented us with a dazzling explanation of the gospel of righteousness-revealed. What lesson does he draw? "Boasting … is excluded" (v 27).

No boasting

Read Romans 3:27-30

What you "boast" in is what gives you confidence to go out and face the day. It is the thing of which you say, *I am a somebody because I have that. I can manage what today brings because I am this.* What you boast in is what fundamentally defines you; it is where you draw your identity from.

- ❓ *Why would being saved by observing the law (v 27) enable someone to boast?*

- ❓ *But we are justified by "faith" (v 27). Why does this exclude all boasting (v 27)?*

This is more challenging than it may at first appear. Paul is saying we must give up all our sense of identity and security, all our grounds of dignity and self-worth—because "a person is justified by faith apart from … the law" (v 28). Whether we are religious (circumcised Jews) or not (uncircumcised Gentiles), there is one God, and one way to be right with him—through faith (v 29-30). To stop boasting is to realise that our best achievements have done nothing to justify us, and that our worst failings do not exclude us.

Apply

- ❓ *What are the aspects of your life or character that you find easiest to boast*

about, to rely on, to look to, in which to find your sense of worth?

- ❓ *How and where do they, or could they, let you down?*

- ❓ *How will you replace that boasting with boasting only "in the cross of our Lord Jesus Christ" (Galatians 6:14)?*

We are not to be self-confident, but Christ-confident. This means we face the day (even the day of our death) saying, *I have Christ. His death means I am God's child. World, I need nothing from you, and you can take nothing from me. I have Christ.*

Uphold the law

Read Romans 3:31

- ❓ *Why might someone think that faith "nullifies" the law?*

How does faith in Christ "uphold" the law? First, because it shows the law must be kept in order to be righteous—in Christ's life, it was. Second, it shows that law-breaking will be punished—in Christ's death, it was. Third, it enables us to love the beauty of the law rather than hating it. If we are obeying to be saved, we will either change the law to make keeping it easier, or be crushed by the law because keeping it is impossible. Only the gospel allows us to care about justice and know we are forgiven.

More on righteousness

Paul now calls two witnesses to support his case: the founder of the Jewish nation, and the greatest king of the Jewish nation.

Read Romans 4:1-16

An extremely important word in this section is *logizdomai*, translated "credited" (v 3, 4, 5, 6, 9, 11) and "counted" (v 8). To "credit" something is to confer a status on it that was not there before.

How it came

❓ *What does the Scripture say Abraham "discovered" (v 1) about how to be right with God (v 3)?*

❓ *How does Paul describe the kind of person whom God makes righteous (v 5)?*

This does not mean a saved person does not obey the law, but that they no longer trust in obeying the law ("work") *to be saved*. They transfer their trust from themselves and their efforts instead to God and his promises.

···· TIME OUT ····

❓ *How is this kind of faith different from "believing in God"?*

❓ *What did King David discover about being someone to whom God had credited righteousness (v 6-8)?*

Pray

Confess your sins to God openly and honestly, knowing that he forgives them all.

Apply

It is revealing to ask ourselves, *Why will I get into heaven?* Anything that relies on us, or even our faith (e.g. *Because I am trying to be good* or *Because I believe in God with all my heart*) is not saving faith, because it relies on me. Abraham would have answered, *Because God has promised to save me, and he keeps his promises.*

❓ *How would you answer that question?*

When it came

❓ *What question does Paul pose in verse 9?*

❓ *Why does this matter to us today, if we are not Jewish?*

If Abraham was circumcised before he was made righteous, we could say that faith + circumcision = right with God.

❓ *But what is in fact the case (v 9b-11)?*

If Abraham obeyed the law before he was made righteous, we could say that faith + obedience = right with God. But the law was given centuries after Abraham died...

❓ *What is in fact the case (v 13)?*

❓ *Why is verse 16 both a good summary of this section, and very exciting for believers today?*

He believed God

What does it mean to believe God? Here, Paul outlines from the life of Abraham what saving faith is.

Read Romans 4:17-25

❓ *How does Paul describe who God is (v 17)?*

And this was the God whom Abraham knew, and trusted, and lived for...

Abraham believed

❓ *What did Abraham do (v 18)?*

❓ *Why was doing this "against all hope", does verse 19 reveal?*

❓ *But, despite the apparently impossible nature of the promises, what was Abraham confident about (v 21)?*

Abraham did not simply believe God existed, or that he was good and holy. To "believe God" is to look at what God has said and to let that define reality for you. It means...

• not going on feelings or appearances (v 19). Abraham looked at his and his wife's bodies, and the idea of having a son was impossible. But he didn't go on appearances, nor trust in himself; he trusted God.

• focusing on facts about God. "God had power" (v 21). Abraham knew God had created everything; so he had the power to create life in Sarah's womb. Faith is not the absence of thinking; it is thinking hard about God and what is true about him.

• trusting the word of God. "God had power to do what he had promised" (v 21). Believ-ing God is to trust and live by what he has promised—taking him at his word even when feelings, popular opinions or common sense seem to contradict his promise.

And this is the faith that God credits as righteousness (v 22).

We believe

Abraham is an example to us (v 23-24a).

❓ *What "believing" does God credit as righteousness today (v 24b-25)?*

Abraham's faith was in God's promise of a descendant; ours is in the achievement of one of Abraham's descendants.

☑ Apply

❓ *How much does the death and resurrection of the Lord Jesus, and the justification it has achieved, define your reality? How could it do so more?*

❓ *Reflect on your own journey to faith, and your Christian life since then. How have you seen, in your own experience, that God is "the God who gives life to the dead" (v 17)?*

⌃ Pray

Thank God that he can do the impossible; that he has justified you; and that he always keeps his promises. Pray that these truths would define your reality today.

Bible in a year: 2 Chronicles 5 • Psalm 134 • Proverbs 14 – 15 ⬇

The joy of justification

If we are justified, we will one day be in God's eternal kingdom; a wonderful future lies ahead of us. But Paul wants us also to appreciate the benefits justification brings now.

Since we are justified

Read Romans 5:1-2

It helps to know that "peace with God" is not the same as "peace *of* God". It is not a feeling, but a state. And "glory of God" refers to his perfect, wonderful presence.

> ❓ *What benefits of being justified does Paul lay out here (try to put them in your own words)?*

> ❓ *Without being justified, the opposite of each of these is true of us. How does remembering this help us to appreciate still further the benefits of justification?*

But Paul then anticipates an objection: *This is all very well... but right now I am experiencing real pain. What good are these things when I am suffering?*

Even in suffering

Read Romans 5:3-5

> ❓ *What is remarkable about what Paul says about our sufferings (v 3)?*

> ❓ *What is it that Christians "know", which means they can view suffering like this (v 3-5)? (Note: It helps to know that "character" means "testedness".)*

"Hope" here means a stronger assurance of our peace with God, our access to God and our future home in glory. The benefits of justification are not only not diminished by suffering, they are enlarged by it.

If I am trying to be justified by works, then suffering will crush me—I will feel that I am being punished for my sins; or it will make me proud—I will think that my suffering means I deserve future blessing. Suffering will drive me away from God, or towards self-reliance.

But if I am justified by faith, then I know that I am at peace with God, that I can speak to him as my Father, and that I will one day see his face. And I know that my suffering has a purpose; that it is detaching me from things I could place my hope in, and encouraging me to place my hope in the only place that can bear my hopes eternally: God himself. Now I can rejoice in my suffering, because my joys remain joys in my sorrow.

···· TIME OUT ···

Think back to a time of suffering in your life (perhaps it is happening right now).

> ❓ *Did that time draw you away from God, or drive you deeper into faith in him?*

🔼 Pray

Thank God that, as his child, you can rejoice even as you suffer. Pray that the truth of justification by faith would make this kind of difference to your experience of life. Speak to him about any areas where you are suffering now, that you would cling onto the truths, and joy, of verses 3-5.

Loved and assured

How do we know God loves us? How can we really know we will be in eternity with him?

Double evidence

Read Romans 5:5-8

❓ *What is the first way in which we know God loves us (v 5)?*

This is an internal, subjective ground of assurance of God's love. Paul's language shows that it can be quite a strong experience, though it can also be mild and gentle (which is more common). It is the *experience* of having hope (i.e. certainty) that we are justified in Christ.

···· TIME OUT ····································

❓ *How have you experienced this kind of heart-knowledge of God's love?*

···

❓ *What is the second way Paul says we know God loves us (v 6)?*

People rarely die for those who see themselves as good (v 7a); sometimes people will die for someone who is truly good (v 7b).

❓ *But what were we like when Christ died for us (v 8)?*

❓ *How does the fact that he was the Christ, and we were like this, demonstrate just how much God loves us?*

This is objective, concrete evidence of God's love for you. You can look back to a day in history, and point at a man dying on a cross, and know that God loves you.

Our future

Read Romans 5:9-11

❓ *What, does Paul remind us, has Christ already done?*

❓ *What can we therefore be sure Christ will do?*

Signs of rejoicing

What are the signs of rejoicing in your friendship (reconciliation) with God, through the justification Christ has won you? Here are four:

1. Your mind is deeply satisfied with the doctrine of justification by faith. You enjoy thinking and speaking about it.
2. When you discover in yourself a new flaw, the discovery doesn't make you doubt God's love; instead, it makes his grace more precious to you.
3. When you sin, you don't try to excuse your performance, or make up for it. You know your best wouldn't merit acceptance by God, and your worst does not jeopardise it.
4. When you face death, you do so calmly, because you are going to a Friend.

🔼 Pray

Use these four signs of rejoicing to thank God for justifying you; and then pray that your outlook and life would display these signs more and more.

The King forsaken

All of King David's psalms point us to Jesus, the ultimate King, in one way or another. But some do so in very unmissable and striking ways—none more so than this one.

Anguish expressed

Read Psalm 22:1-21

❓ *Why is it so surprising—even shocking—that this is a psalm written by Israel's king?*

Jesus quoted verse 1 as he hung on the cross (see Matthew 27:46), showing that it speaks of him and his situation.

❓ *Look again through Psalm 22:1-21. Why would Jesus understand it that way?*

❓ *Read 2 Corinthians 5:21. What does it mean that Jesus was "forsaken" by God (Psalm 22:1)? Why was he forsaken?*

❓ *How do these verses help you to understand and appreciate more deeply what Jesus endured for you?*

🔼 Pray

Take a minute or two to praise and thank Jesus that he faced the shame and agony of the cross for you and in your place.

Hope affirmed

Read Psalm 22:22-31

In these verses, the forsaken king looks beyond his affliction to what lies ahead. He knows that suffering, shame, abandonment and death are not the end of the road. When we take that on board, we realise that when Jesus quoted this psalm on the cross, he was not only expressing his anguish—he was also affirming his hope.

❓ *The king has asked God for rescue. What does he expect the response to be?*

❓ *What will he do in response?*

The king has spoken of being abandoned and rejected. But now he speaks of having a "people" (v 22).

❓ *What will the future look like for the king's people?*

···· TIME OUT ·································

The writer of Hebrews quotes Psalm 22:22 in Hebrews 2:12, in a section where he is talking about the significance of Jesus becoming a real human being. We can see why the writer would choose to quote Psalm 22: it shows so very clearly the fact that Jesus suffered as a real human being, and plumbed the very depths of the experience of human pain.

Read Hebrews 2:10-18

❓ *Why is it so important that Jesus lived, suffered and died as a real human?*

Jesus has declared his name and the praises of God to us (Psalm 22:22) in the gospel. He has fulfilled his role from the psalm.

❓ *How does the psalm teach us to respond to his suffering, death and resurrection?*

🔼 Pray

Once more, thank Jesus for all he has done, and will do, for you.

Two humanities

The previous verses prompt a question: how can one man's sacrifice, as noble as it was, bring about such incredible benefits to so many?

In Adam

Read Romans 5:12-14

❓ *How did sin and death enter the world (v 12)?*

Paul is talking about Adam, the first man.

❓ *What does he say happened when Adam sinned in the Garden of Eden (end of verse 12)?*

The sense of the Greek translated as "because all sinned" shows that Paul is referring to a single, past action. Paul is not simply saying that we all sin *like* Adam, but that we all sinned *in* Adam. So, he says in verses 13-14, whether or not people had God's law, everyone died, because everyone was guilty for what Adam did. "Death reigned" (v 14).

Paul is teaching the truth that humanity has a representative—a federal head. Whatever that "head" achieves or loses, we all achieve or lose. One example of a federal head is a president or prime minister. If they declare war, then all their countrymen are at war. If they make peace, then the whole country is at peace. What they do, the nation does.

Before God, Adam is humanity's representative, our federal head. We are dealt with according to what he did. So when he sinned, "death came to all men, because all sinned" (v 12).

In Christ

Read Romans 5:15-21

❓ *Who is the other federal head introduced in verse 15?*

Adam is a "pattern" of Christ, "the one to come" (v 14), in that both are the federal head of a humanity; the merits or otherwise of what they do are transferred to their people.

❓ *What does being part of Adam's race bring (v 16-19)?*

❓ *What does being part of Christ's humanity bring (v 16-19)?*

The late John Stott summed it up well: "Whether we are condemned or justified depends on which humanity we belong to ... the old humanity initiated by Adam, or to the new humanity initiated by Christ".

These verses teach us that, if Christ is our representative, whatever is true of him is, in God's sight, true of us.

Think about what Jesus is like; where he is; what he does. In God's eyes, all these things are true of you.

⌃ Pray

Thank God for Jesus' active obedience in his life and death. Thank God that he deals with you through a federal head, so that Christ's life and death are your life and death.

Union with Christ

Next, Paul deals with some objections to the gospel of righteousness-received, which he poses as four questions. Today and tomorrow, we're looking at the first.

The question

Read Romans 6:1

❓ *What is the objection?*

In one sense, what Paul is about to do is simply to re-explain and re-apply the doctrine of our "union" with Christ—the truth that all that is true of Christ is true of his people—which he outlined in 5:12-21. But in another sense, this question introduces a new section of the letter. Chapters 1 – 5 told us what God *has* accomplished for us in the gospel; chapters 6 – 8 tell us what God *will* accomplish in us through the gospel.

The answer

Read Romans 6:2

❓ *What has happened to a Christian?*

❓ *What should a Christian no longer do?*

"Died to sin" does not mean that we no longer can sin, or no longer want to sin (as chapter 7 will show). It means that the moment someone becomes a Christian, they are no longer under the reign, the power and control of sin.

So to "live in it" (i.e. sin) does not mean to sin (otherwise, everyone would "live in it"). It means "to swim in it", to let it be the main driver of your life. So to "live in sin" means to tolerate it, rather than grieve it; and to make no progress with it, rather than to fight it.

The doctrine

Read Romans 6:3-5

❓ *What happened when you became a Christian (v 3-4—Paul uses the word "baptised" here to mean conversion)?*

❓ *What will happen to you because you have been "united with him" (v 5)?*

This is a breathtaking outlining of the doctrine of union with Christ. If we trust Jesus, we are "in him"—whatever is true of him is now legally true of us. When he died, we actually died. When he rose, we actually rose.

❓ *Why is this the beginning of an answer to the idea, "Christ has saved me, so I can sin more"?*

⌄ Apply

Though you may obey sin, and at times you will obey sin, the fact is that you no longer have to obey sin.

❓ *How does this both encourage and challenge you?*

❓ *Is there any area of your life where you are in danger of "living in sin"?*

The truth, if you are a Christian, is that you are united with Christ—your sinful old self died with him, and you've been raised to new life with him.

❓ *How will this motivate you not to live in the old way any longer?*

If we died with Christ

In these verses, Paul is continuing to explain our status in Christ, and how that has changed our relationship to sin.

You died

Read Romans 6:6-7

> ❷ *If you are a Christian, what has happened to the old "you" (v 6)?*
>
> ❷ *What is the consequence of this (v 6)?*

The "old self" and the "body ruled by sin" are not the same thing. The first is the pre-Christian "me". And so Paul is saying that that person is dead. They died when Jesus died. There is now a completely new "me". But the body of sin still exists, because that is sin expressing itself through our bodies.

So while sin remains in us with a lot of strength, it no longer controls our personalities and lives. That person who could do nothing other than sin has died, and "has been set free from sin". So while we still have bodies which sin, sinful behaviour goes against our deepest self-understanding, against our identity.

Imagine a wicked military force had complete control of a country, and a good army invaded and took power and threw the wicked army out of the capital and seat of government. The wicked force was out of power, defeated, but still able to create havoc in the rest of the country, as a guerrilla force. So with the Christian—sin has been thrown out of power, and has no hold over us, yet it still fights hard.

You live

Read Romans 6:8-14

> ❷ *What do we know lies ahead of us, and why (v 8-9)?*

Jesus bore and dealt with sin once and for all in his death; his life beyond death is about living for God (v 11).

> ❷ *How should we respond to that truth (v 11)?*
>
> ❷ *What does this mean we must not do; and what does it mean we must do (v 12-13)?*

We have "died to sin" (v 2); so why does Paul tell us to "count yourselves dead to sin" (v 11)? Because being dead to sin is like a privilege, or legal right. We have to act on this privilege, and live in light of this truth. Otherwise, we are like someone with financial difficulties who inherits a huge trust fund, but doesn't withdraw any money from it. It is only as we live as people who are dead to sin and alive to God that we will experience a life free from the power of sin.

▾ Apply

> ❷ *Where is your fight with sin particularly hard at the moment?*
>
> ❷ *How would remembering what has happened to your old self, and who you are now in Christ, help you next time the battle is raging?*

The freedom of slavery

Having died with Christ, a Christian has been "set free from sin" (v 7) and is no longer "under the law" (v 14). So aren't we now free to live any way we choose?.

Slaves of…

Read Romans 6:15-18

❓ *What two things can someone offer themselves to as slaves (v 16)?*

❓ *How does Paul describe a Christian's conversion in terms of slavery (v 17-18)?*

No one is free. Everyone is a slave to something or someone! We all offer ourselves as sacrifices on some altar, serve some cause, and slave for what we see as our highest good in life. What we serve becomes our master; it controls our actions and attitudes.

And Paul says there are fundamentally only two kinds of masters: God (obedience and righteousness) or sin. Whenever we choose not to obey God, we are not choosing to be free; we are choosing to be slaves to sin, rather than our Saviour.

⌵ Apply

❓ *Is this different to the way you usually think of your choices in life? How?*

❓ *Think back to last time you chose to disobey God. How were you offering yourself as a slave to sin at that point?*

The two slaveries

Paul contrasts these two slaveries in terms of their origin, their development, and their results. First, he says "you used to be slaves to sin" (v 17)—this is what we are by nature.

It begins automatically; we are born into it. But when you "obey[ed] from your heart the … teaching" (v 17—i.e. the gospel), we became slaves of God. This slavery begins when we are converted.

Read Romans 6:19-23

❓ *What happens as someone lives in slavery to sin (v 19)?*

❓ *What about as someone lives in slavery to righteousness (v 19)?*

As we act in a particular way, with a particular motivation, it shapes our character, and it becomes more natural and obvious to us to act that way again.

❓ *What is the result of slavery to sin (v 21, 23)?*

Paul is not only talking about eternal future death, but a present death—a "death" people "reap at that time" (v 21). It is a kind of death in life—a brokenness. If we are enslaved to something other than God, we won't reap satisfaction and security, but anxiety, self-pity, a sense of inadequacy, envy, and so on.

❓ *What is the result of slavery to God (v 23)?*

⌵ Apply

❓ *How do you need to apply verse 19 today?*

❓ *Someone says to you, "I don't want to be a Christian because you have to give up your freedom". What would you say?*

Bible in a year: Ecclesiastes 10 – 12 • 1 Corinthians 4

Not just slaves

Paul has been using the imagery of slavery to explain our relationship to God and to sin. Now, he switches the analogy …

Till death us do part

Read Romans 7:1-3

❓ *What relationship is Paul now talking about, and what does he say about it (v 2-3)?*

❓ *What stops a marriage being binding?*

Marriage after death

Read Romans 7:4-6

All of us were once "married" to—bound by—the law. It was not a good husband, because we could not satisfy it, and (as we'll see more of in the next studies) the "sinful passions aroused by the law were at work" (v 5). The law brought out the worst in us.

❓ *So what did being married to the law result in (end of v 5)?*

❓ *But what has now happened, and how (v 4)?*

In Paul's image in verses 2-3, it was the husband's death that freed the wife to remarry. In our case, it is our death in Christ that frees us to "remarry".

❓ *Who do we now belong to (v 4)?*

What an incredible metaphor—we are married to Christ! To be a Christian is to fall in love with Jesus and to enter into a legal yet personal relationship as comprehensive as marriage. No part of your life goes unaffected.

After all, marriage entails a significant loss of freedom and independence. If you are married, you cannot live as you choose; you have a duty and an obligation. But you also have the possibility of love, intimacy, acceptance and security that you could not have outside marriage. So the loss of freedom in marriage is a joy, not a burden. In a good marriage, your whole life is affected and changed by the wishes and desires of the person you love. You get pleasure from pleasing them. You discover what their wishes are, and then you make changes in order to fulfil those wishes.

So here, Paul gives us the ultimate answer to why Christians obey God. We do it because we are slaves of his, rather than of sin; we also do it because we want to please the one who saved us, to whom we now belong. Obeying the law is a way to please the one we love. So obedience becomes a joy, not a burden.

⌃ Pray

Thank God that he has freed you from slavery and marriage to the law through your death in Christ. Thank God for the new life you now have, with him as your Master and Christ as your Husband. Speak to him about ways in which you are still living as though sin and the law were in charge of you, and ask for his help to live as the new person you now are.

Is the law sin?

When we were "married" to the law, our "sinful passions [were] aroused by the law …
so that we bore fruit for death" (v 5). So the law, it seems, is sinful and deadly.

Read Romans 7:7-12

When we read the law

❷ *How does Paul answer the idea that the law itself is sin (v 7)?*

❷ *What is the purpose of the law (v 7)?*

❷ *Why is it a good thing that the law does this (think back to 3:20-21)?*

As we look at the law, it exposes our sin. But that's not all...

❷ *As Paul read the command "Do not covet", what did his sinful nature do (7:8)?*

Paul is saying that in him—and in each of us—there is a desire to do something for no other reason than because it is forbidden. The law exposes our sin; our sin exploits the law to cause us to sin.

How we see ourselves

Paul says (v 9) that he was "alive apart from the law". He is probably talking about his self-perception before he became a Christian. Because he had never really thought about what the law really required—because he saw it as a behavioural code which he could keep externally—he felt he was spiritually alive, acceptable to God.

❷ *But then what happened (v 9)?*

Now his self-perception was right—he was dead, a moral failure, unable to save

himself. And it was the command not to covet that "killed" him. Coveting is to be discontent with what God has given you and bitter about what he has given others. This command cannot be reduced to an external behaviour—it is all about a heart attitude.

So here's what happened to Paul. He read and reflected on this command; and as he did so, his sin prompted him to covet. And he realised that he was not a law-keeper; he was a sinner.

What the law is

❷ *What does Paul conclude about the law (v 12)?*

The law is not sinful—but Paul is, and so are we. Our sin uses the law to prompt us to sin. That's why "the very commandment that was intended to bring life actually [brings] death" (v 10).

⌃ Pray

Thank God for his law, which shows you what is good and godly.

Confess ways in which you have been convicted of your sin recently by God's word.

Ask God to show you ways in which your sinfulness is exploiting your Bible-reading to tempt you to sin.

Thank God that, once you know you are "dead", you can find life through faith in Jesus' obedience on your behalf.

Ultimate protection

We have come to the most famous psalm of all. And there's good reason for its fame: it is beautiful, full of great comfort, and addresses us in every season of life.

The dream behind Britain's National Insurance scheme was to provide comprehensive protection and care for the whole population, "from the cradle to the grave". Many other nations' governments have similar initiatives. Here, David reminds us that in the Lord our shepherd, we enjoy protection and care that cannot be matched by any human scheme or institution, stretching even beyond the grave.

Read Psalm 23

The pasture

Re-read Psalm 23:1-4

The Bible describes the Lord in many ways—as a parent, a warrior, a king and a judge. Here he is described as a shepherd.

> ❷ *What does that tell you about the Lord?*

> ❷ *As shepherd of his people, what does the Lord do in these verses?*

David speaks of going through the "darkest valley" (v 4) and knowing the Lord's protection and care even then.

⌄ Apply

Think about threatening or unsettling things that are going on in your life at the moment—in your family, at work, in your community, or in your church.

> ❷ *What is the impact in these situations of knowing the Lord as your shepherd?*

The banquet hall

Re-read Psalm 23:5-6

The imagery moves away from shepherd and pasture to that of host and banquet hall.

Back in verse 4, David was under threat and in danger; now (v 5) he is enjoying a feast in the presence of his enemies. These enemies may still be threatening the Lord's people, or they may be captives at a victory supper.

> ❷ *Either way, why is it significant that the Lord provides a feast for his people in the midst of their enemies? What does this demonstrate?*

David insists not only that the Lord's "goodness and love" are available to him all the time, but that the Lord actually *chases* him with his goodness and love (v 6).

> ❷ *Why is it such a comfort to know that the Lord's "goodness and love" pursue you through life?*

⌄ Apply

The greatest security in life comes from the final line of the psalm, which every believer can take to their lips: "I will dwell in the house of the Lord for ever" (v 6).

> ❷ *Do you view all your challenges, trials and difficulties in the light of that hope?*

> ❷ *If you did that today, what difference might it make to you?*

⌄

Our internal battle

We now come to one of the most remarkable and honest passages in the whole of the Bible.

Read Romans 7:13-25

···· TIME OUT ·····························

Many thoughtful people have argued Paul must be talking here of his experience as an unbeliever. But it is much more likely he is talking as a Christian. The verbs are present tense; he says, "I delight in God's law" (v 22), which is something only a Christian can do (see 8:7); and he knows he is lost but that Jesus will rescue him (7:24-25).

Two Pauls

- ❓ *What is Paul like in his "inner being" (v 22)?*
- ❓ *But what else is he like (v 23)?*
- ❓ *What is the consequence (v 15, 19)?*

We all have, in some sense, multiple selves—sometimes we want to be this, sometimes we want to be that. We all face the question, *Which is my true, real self?*

For a Christian, that question is settled, even though the conflict isn't. In our inner selves—in our heart of hearts—we love God, and his law, and desire to live his way. But, as we saw four days ago, there is still a powerful centre of sin remaining in us— our "sinful nature" (7:5, NIV84), or "flesh" (ESV, NIV2011). Paul says it seeks "what I hate" (v 15)—and so, he says, "I have the desire to do what is good, but I cannot carry it out" (v 18).

Apply

- ❓ *Do you recognise this experience of inner struggle in your own Christian life?*
- ❓ *How do you deal with it?*

Two cries

- ❓ *What is Paul's conclusion about himself (v 24a)? Why is it accurate?*
- ❓ *Why is this cry of despair not the only thing his heart cries out (v 24b-25a)?*

These are the two cries of the Christian's heart. Paul is honest about what he is like; but he also remembers what God is like. Christ has rescued Paul from the penalty for sin at the cross, and will one day rescue him from the presence of sin when he returns. **Read Romans 8:10-11.**

Apply

- ❓ *How does knowing that Paul struggled with sin like this comfort you today?*
- ❓ *Do you tend to excuse your sin, rather than acknowledge your wretchedness? Or do you tend to forget to look beyond your own failings to Christ's rescue?*

Pray

Heavenly Father, I am wretched. Thank you so, so much for rescuing me through Christ Jesus. Amen.

Right with God

Today is an opportunity to look back over Romans 1 – 7, and enjoy and reflect on the great promises God makes to his people in these wonderful chapters.

For each set of verses, reflect on these questions:

- ❓ *What am I being promised here?*
- ❓ *What am I being told here about what it means to be a Christian?*
- ❓ *If I believe this more deeply, what about my heart or my life will change?*

Space has been left to scribble down your answers and thoughts if you want to.

How righteousness is offered

Read Romans 1:2-4, 17; 3:20-26

How righteousness comes

Read Romans 1:17; 3:22; 4:16; 6:3-5

How righteousness changes us

Read Romans 5:1-5; 6:1-2, 11-13; 7:22-25a

In chapter 4, we saw that Abraham discovered that God is "the God who gives life to the dead and calls into being things that were not" (4:17).

- ❓ *How is this a good summary of all that Paul has told us God has done for us and in us?*
- ❓ *How have you seen God doing these things in your life?*

 Pray

Thank God for the truths that have particularly struck you and encouraged you from Romans 1 – 7.

JEREMIAH: Are you ready?

What does God say to a declining, struggling church? God sent Jeremiah to a diminishing nation—to tell them things were going to get worse before they got better.

God's word came

Read Jeremiah 1:1-3

❓ *What are we told about Jeremiah?*

❓ *What significant event happened at the end of his ministry (v 3)?*

Jeremiah spoke God's words from about 627 BC until 586 BC. The mention of God's judgment on his people at the end of his ministry indicates the tone—and degree of "success"—of Jeremiah's preaching.

Read Jeremiah 1:4-10

❓ *When did God choose to appoint Jeremiah as his spokesman (v 5)?*

❓ *How does God respond to Jeremiah's objection (v 6-8)?*

❓ *What is Jeremiah's role (v 9-10)?*

God appoints Jeremiah using images from farming (uproot and plant), building (tear down and build) and warfare (destroy and overthrow). In the book we're going to read, there is both judgment and hope—but more judgment than hope. God needs to clear the weeds before he can plant his crops. He will demolish the ruins before rebuilding his city.

⌄ Apply

Read Matthew 28:18-20

God repeatedly calls us to serve him in roles we are not ready for. But he gives us

his most frequent command ("Do not be afraid", 28:10) and his most precious promise ("I am with you", 28:20).

❓ *How has God kept this promise in the past when you've served him in ways you didn't feel ready for?*

❓ *Are there any ways today God is calling you to do something you don't feel ready for?*

❓ *How do his promises here help you to obey today?*

Judgment is coming

Read Jeremiah 1:11-20

❓ *What is going to happen to God's people (the tribe of Judah and their capital city, Jerusalem, v 14-15)?*

❓ *Why is this going to happen (v 16)?*

Jeremiah's message is not an easy one for him to speak (v 17-18) or often for us to hear. But it's God's message—for the people who heard him preach, for the survivors in exile who first read this book, and for us today.

❓ *How has this chapter prepared you to hear Jeremiah's difficult message?*

⌃ Pray

Pray that you will listen to God's word in Jeremiah with humility and reverence; and that you won't be afraid to speak Jesus' words to others even if you don't feel ready.

He says, she says

Have you ever heard a couple on the edge of break-up arguing about whose fault it is? We listen in to one of those arguments between the Lord and his bride, Israel.

Honeymoon

This is the first sermon that God gives Jeremiah to preach. He starts with a bang!

Read Jeremiah 2:1-3

❓ *What was God's relationship with Israel like at first?*

It started so well! As always, the true tragedy of sin isn't just broken rules, but a broken relationship with God.

Adultery

Read Jeremiah 2:4-19

❓ *How has God treated Israel (v 5-7)?*
❓ *How has Israel treated God (v 10-13)?*
❓ *How does Jeremiah show the stupidity of this betrayal?*

A cistern (v 13) is a hole dug in rock to hold rainwater. Even when they work, they aren't as refreshing as a spring, but Israel's cisterns don't even hold water. Their replacement gods let them down.

❓ *What broken cisterns do people—do you—dig today?*

Quarrels

Read Jeremiah 2:20-37

❓ *What does Israel have to say for herself?*
❓ *What effect does God's barrage of questions have?*

❓ *How has Israel used God (v 27-28)?*

Israel pleads "not guilty" (v 23, 35), but the people have been caught red-handed (v 26). Only one partner in this marriage has been unfaithful. Israel may say, *God won't judge us, we're his bride* but they were an adulterous bride heading for a divorce.

✔ Apply

In the New Testament, the church is the bride of Christ (e.g. Revelation 21:2). But are we any more faithful to our divine Husband?

Read Revelation 2:1-7

The church in Ephesus had sound doctrine, busy ministry programmes and a track record of faithfulness (v 2-3).

❓ *But what was missing (v 4)?*
❓ *What did Jesus call them to do (v 5)?*
❓ *Might you, or your church, have forsaken the love for Jesus you had when you first turned to Christ? Do you use him or love him?*

⌃ Pray

Ask for God's forgiveness if you have forsaken him and lost your love for him. Thank him that Jesus was forsaken on the cross so that God would not forsake you. Pray that you and your church would be so amazed by his love for you that you would grow in your love for him.

Mending broken hearts

Is there any hope for a marriage after one partner has committed adultery? Is there any hope for a relationship with God after Israel has committed spiritual adultery?

Jeremiah's answer to both questions is, "Yes—but only if there is heartfelt repentance". The key word is turn/return.

Repentance needed

Read Jeremiah 3:1-11

God's OT law banned a husband and wife reuniting after divorce and remarriage (compare verse 1 with Deuteronomy 24:1-4).

> ❓ *What is Judah's continued attitude towards the Lord (Jeremiah 3:2-5)?*

No relationship can survive that sort of sorry/not sorry attitude.

> ❓ *Why is Judah's adultery more blameworthy than Israel's (v 6-11)?*

> ❓ *What is the difference between returning to God in heart and doing so only in pretence (v 10)?*

Repentance is blessed

Read Jeremiah 3:11-25

> ❓ *How is the Lord different to Israel and Judah (v 12)?*

> ❓ *What does he call on them to do (v 13-14)?*

> ❓ *What does he promise if they do this (v 15-18)?*

With humans there can be no return, but there can be with God. The only thing stopping these promises being a reality is the people's continued unfaithfulness (v 19-25).

What repentance is

Read Jeremiah 4:1-4

> ❓ *How should repentance be...*
> - *personal (v 1a)?* • *vertical (v 1b)?*
> - *horizontal (v 2)?* • *internal (v 3-4)?*

We are tempted to plaster over the problem of sin. We might repent of one sin but not another. We might pray and attend church but not stop sinning. We might conform outwardly but not love the Lord with all our hearts. That is to try to have Jesus alongside our idols of family, career, comfort, nation and so on, rather than letting him be supreme over them. But sin must be rooted out; we need to clear out the old weeds of sin and start all over again with him (v 3-4).

☑ Apply

Deuteronomy 10:16 and 30:6 promised that God would change his people's hearts.

Read Romans 2:28-29

> ❓ *How can our hearts be circumcised?*

> ❓ *How does your typical response to your sin measure up to Jeremiah's call to true repentance?*

Praise God that in his grace there is a way back to relationship with him after our unfaithfulness. Pray that the Spirit would circumcise your heart so that you love the Lord with undivided devotion.

Bible in a year: 2 Chronicles 13 – 15 • 1 Kings 15

You have been warned

Warnings require action. When the air-raid siren sounds, get to a shelter; when the fire alarm rings, get out of the building; when the fuel indicator flashes, fill up.

God's warnings require action too.

This long section starts with God's air-raid siren—"Sound the trumpet!"—because an invading army is being sent by God (4:1-8). It alternates between announcements of disaster and destruction (4:9-17, 19-21, 23-31; 5:14-17) and the reasons for this punishment (4:18, 22; 5:1-13, 18-31). Read them if you have time! The climax comes in chapter 6.

Listen to the warning!

Read Jeremiah 6:1-8

❷ *What disaster is Jeremiah warning them about (v 1-5)?*

❷ *Who is in command of this army (v 6-7)?*

❷ *How should Jerusalem respond (v 8)?*

Jeremiah gives accurate warnings but nobody will listen to him, however desperately he cries out.

Who will listen?

Read Jeremiah 6:9-15

❷ *How do people respond to Jeremiah's warnings (v 10)?*

❷ *What explanations are we given for why they won't listen (v 13-15)?*

The people are like children sticking their fingers in their ears and shouting, "I can't hear you!" They hate being told to change their ways (v 10).

Read Jeremiah 6:16-20

❷ *How can the people avoid the approaching disaster (v 16)?*

❷ *How do they respond instead (v 16-19)?*

These people spend huge amounts of money apparently worshipping the Lord (v 20), but they don't listen to his words or change their lives to obey what he has said. Therefore there will be no escape (v 21-26).

Read Jeremiah 6:27-30

If no one listens to Jeremiah's preaching, we might think he has been a failure. But these verses explain the role God has given him. He is a tester of metals, and his warnings reveal the hearts of his listeners.

❷ *How might that change what we see as "success" in preaching today?*

☑ Apply

Read Matthew 11:28-30

❷ *How does Jesus apply the promise and command from Jeremiah 6:16?*

God's message always contains invitations ("You will find rest for your souls") and warnings ("I am bringing disaster").

❷ *How are you responding to them?*

❷ *Who would you like to share the warning and invitation with this week?*

Pray for an opportunity to do so.

Not all about me

The heart of Christianity doesn't focus on me and my often mediocre performance for God. It is about trusting in Jesus and his perfect achievements for us.

That's as true of the Psalms as it is of the Gospels. Sometimes the emphasis is on looking to our glorious leader—the fulfilment of all that King David promised. At other times there is more emphasis on what it is like to follow Jesus. But always the psalms point us to Christ and encourage us to follow.

Immense power

Read Psalm 24:1-2

I hate being told what to do. Whether it is by parents, teachers, a boss or a church leader, none of us like being told what to do.

❷ *According to these verses, what gives God the right to tell us what to do?*

Pure standards

Read Psalm 24:3-6

"The mountain of the Lord" refers to the place where God symbolically dwells and rules. In Old Testament times it pointed particularly to Mount Zion, where the temple stood in Jerusalem.

❷ *What are the requirements for approaching God in these verses?*

❷ *What do you think is meant by "clean hands and a pure heart"?*

❷ *So who can come into God's presence? Who is pure enough to meet the standards of verses 3-6 and approach God?*

Ever since the fall, the way to God has been barred. A flaming sword at the entrance to Eden (Genesis 3:24), and then a thick curtain at the entrance to the Most Holy Place in the temple (Exodus 26:33) kept sinful people away from the holy God.

The King of glory

The last section pictures a crowd buzzing with anticipation, craning their necks for a glimpse of the approaching figure.

Read Psalm 24:7-10

So who is this King of glory? How can he ascend the hill of the Lord and at the same time *be* "the Lord"? **Read Psalm 2:6-7**—it's because this King is God's divine Son. A thousand years after this psalm, the King of glory led his people back into the presence of God. He did it as he hung on a cross outside the city walls, bearing the punishment for our sins.

When you wonder whether God can accept you or have anything to do with you, remember you don't approach him on the basis of your own "pure" heart. You approach with "confidence ... by the blood of Jesus" (Hebrews 10:19).

⌃ Pray

Turn the psalm into a prayer of your own. Praise God for his greatness in Psalm 24:1-2; confess your sins using v 3-6; praise Jesus for leading us into God's presence in v 7-10.

Safe house?

What does God think of people who proudly call themselves Christians and are sure of God's favour, but make no effort to pursue justice? Are they safe? Are we?

This is Jeremiah's temple sermon—smelling salts to wake us up to the futility of religion without repentance. Verses 3-4 are his two headings: verse 3 is expanded in verses 5-7, and verse 4 in verses 8-15.

Read Jeremiah 7:1-15

Missing obedience

❓ *What must Israel do to carry on living in Jerusalem (v 3)?*

❓ *In what ways do they need to change (v 5-7)?*

The second half of the sermon teaches more on this theme (read it if you have time). The same God who gave commands about sacrifices gave commands about how to live first (v 21-29). Obeying one but not the other is rejecting him. In fact, they don't even obey the ritual commands (v 30-34).

Misplaced trust

For pagans, a temple was the dwelling-place of the local deity, whose presence magically protected the city. But biblical religion is different.

❓ *What do the people of Jerusalem think will keep them safe (v 4)?*

❓ *Why are they not safe (v 8-11)?*

The Lord's house will not keep them safe from their enemies if their actions have made the Lord their enemy! Jeremiah gives

them two historical examples to prove his point.

❓ *What does God say about Shiloh, the place where God's presence dwelled in the days of Samuel (v 12-14)?*

❓ *What happened to Ephraim, the northern half of God's people Israel (v 15)?*

These people are so far gone that God bans Jeremiah from praying for them (v 16-20)! Even the dead will share the judgment of the living (8:1-2) and the living will wish they were dead (8:3).

✔ Apply

Jesus repeated Jeremiah's accusations.

Read Matthew 21:12-13

Calling ourselves God's people and doing religion "right", without ongoing repentance, is just self-deception.

❓ *Are there areas of your life where you're not obeying God's word, while thinking you're ok because you attend church?*

❓ *What would it look like to treat immigrants, orphans and single mothers with justice (Jeremiah 7:5-6)?*

⌃ Pray

Pray that God would grant you a precious faith that works itself out in whole-life, faith-fuelled obedience (2 Peter 1:1-11).

Bible in a year: 1 Kings 17 – 18 • Luke 4 • Jeremiah 10

Wise words

Ever watched someone you love ruin their life through their own stupidity? Then you'll know something of what Jeremiah and the Lord both feel here as they watch Israel.

Wisdom

Read Jeremiah 8:4-13

❷ *How is Israel being stupid (v 4-6)?*

❷ *How do they show they are not as wise as they think (v 7-9)?*

❷ *Why are they not doing the sensible thing and repenting (v 10-13)?*

Weeping

Jeremiah is sometimes known as "the weeping prophet". He points us forward to Jesus, who wept over the suffering and stubbornness of God's people in his day (John 11:35; Luke 19:41-44). In Jeremiah 8 – 9 it is difficult to tell whether it is Jeremiah or the Lord who is expressing their grief.

Read Jeremiah 9:1-11

❷ *Why is the writer so upset (v 1-3)?*

The Israelites have turned lying into an art form (v 4-6). What other option does God have but to judge them (v 7-9)?

❷ *How does Jeremiah show us...*
- *God's grief at judgment (v 10)?*
- *God's commitment to judgment (v 11)?*

❷ *How can you hold both of these together as you think and speak about the God who judges?*

Jeremiah weeps now, but when God's judgment comes it will be the people of Israel who weep and wail (9:12-22).

Wisdom again

How can people escape from the coming calamity? What can we put our confidence in?

Read Jeremiah 9:23-24

❷ *What three things do we tend to boast in, that we think will keep us safe?*

❷ *What one thing should we boast in?*

❷ *What three things does God delight in?*

⌄ Apply

Read 1 Corinthians 1:26-31

True wisdom is still to boast in the Lord and not in our intelligence, power or wealth.

❷ *What is there to boast about in Jesus (v 30-31)?*

❷ *Which do you turn to first when problems arise... your ideas or money or influence, or Jesus?*

❷ *Which do you talk about more to the people around you... your education or purchases or connections, or Jesus?*

⌃ Pray

Confess any ways in which you boast in yourself. Praise God for giving you Jesus as your true wisdom. Pray that you would put your confidence in him and would boast to others about how wise and wonderful he is.

None like the Lord

The stupid sin that was dragging Israel towards disaster was idolatry. In this chapter Jeremiah contrasts the god-frauds with the true Lord.

Senseless idolatry

Read Jeremiah 10:1-16

Verse 2 shows the attraction of idolatry: it's so much easier to fit in with chasing after what everyone else thinks will make them happy, give them meaning and keep them safe. In the West today that can be a partner, a family, a lifestyle, a nation, a career, a position, a reputation—good things that we turn into god-things. Jeremiah shows us how all of these pale in comparison to the true God.

Contrast 1:

- ❓ *Why should we not fear idols (v 3-5)?*
- ❓ *Why should we fear the Lord (v 6-7)?*

Contrast 2:

- ❓ *Why are idols worthless (v 8-9)?*
- ❓ *Why is the Lord worthy of worship (v 10)?*

Contrast 3:

- ❓ *What did the idols not make (v 11)?*
- ❓ *What did the Lord make (v 12-13)?*

Contrast 4:

- ❓ *Why will idols perish (v 14-15)?*
- ❓ *Why will the Lord endure (v 16)?*

Defenceless idolaters

If idols are speechless, powerless, lifeless, useless and bound for judgment, then worshipping them is an insult to God, and brings the same judgment on our own heads.

Read Jeremiah 10:17-25

- ❓ *What does God say he is going to do to those who worship idols (v 17-18)?*
- ❓ *How does Jeremiah intercede for the people (v 23-25)?*

✔ Apply

Think of the people around you: in your family, on your street, at your workplace.

- ❓ *What do they think will make them happy, give them meaning and keep them safe?*
- ❓ *How are you tempted to trust and pursue these things as well?*
- ❓ *Which of the contrasts between the Lord and idols in Jeremiah 10 apply to those idols too?*

✔ Pray

Spend some time praising and worshipping God for who he is, as described in this chapter. Fill your mind and heart with the glorious beauty of his true character, so that you won't be attracted by the idols those around us worship.

Rejected and dejected

Jeremiah faced betrayal, disappointment and confusion. This chapter shows us how he talked to God about this, and how God helped him through it.

A rejected prophet

Some people from Jeremiah's own town, Anathoth, and even from his own family, are plotting to have him killed.

Read Jeremiah 11:18-23

❓ *What pictures does Jeremiah use to describe their actions (v 18-19)?*

❓ *What does he remember about God (v 20)?*

❓ *What does he ask God to do (v 20)?*

❓ *How does God respond to his request (v 21-23)?*

Jeremiah's prayer is similar to many psalms and a model to us: he speaks to God about his feelings, and to his feelings about God (v 20). Both are vital!

Read Jeremiah 12:1-6

❓ *What pictures does Jeremiah use to describe his situation (v 1-2, 4)?*

❓ *What does he remember about God (v 1, 3)?*

❓ *What does he ask God to do (v 3)?*

❓ *How does God respond to his request this time (v 5-6)?*

Maybe God has spotted some self-pity in Jeremiah's heart—and he warns his prophet that it's only going to get worse...

A rejected God

God now speaks in the form of a lament.

Read Jeremiah 12:7-13

Just as Jeremiah was betrayed by his family, the Lord's household has betrayed him.

❓ *What pictures does God use to describe:*
- *how Israel have acted towards him (v 7-9)?*
- *what will happen to Israel (v 9-13)?*

But there is still hope!

Read Jeremiah 12:14-17

There is no favouritism with God. If Israel or any other nation rebel, they are uprooted; if they repent, they are re-planted. He is far more gracious than Jeremiah to those who have betrayed him!

⌃ Pray

Jeremiah had a genuine grievance mixed in with self-pity. In response God promises justice (11:21-23), warns him it will get worse (12:5-6), shares his own rejection (v 7-9) and points him to a wonderful future (v 14-17).

❓ *Are you feeling any justified grief or unjustified self-pity at the moment?*

❓ *How do God's responses to Jeremiah's feelings help you with these?*

❓ *How can you talk to God about these feelings and to these feelings about God?*

Right now would be a great time to start...

Bible in a year: 2 Chronicles 19 – 22

Bound to God

The Lord Jesus' church is meant to reveal his beauty to the world and to bring him glory (e.g. Matthew 5:14-16; Titus 2:10). What happens when it does the opposite?

Unwearable

For Jeremiah's next message, God sends him shopping.

Read Jeremiah 13:1-11

❓ *What did God tell Jeremiah to do with a belt (v 1-6)?*

❓ *What was the belt like at the end (v 7)?*

❓ *How were the people of Judah like that belt (v 8-11)?*

Unbearable

If God's people have become ruined and completely useless, what will he do with them?

Read Jeremiah 13:12-27

❓ *What will happen to the people (v 12-14)?*

❓ *What pictures does he use to describe this judgment?*
• *v 15-16*   • *v 18*
• *v 21-22*   • *v 26-27*

❓ *What hope is there for these people to change (v 23)?*

These are unbearable pictures of judgment and they are difficult for us to read. They were difficult for Jeremiah to speak as well (v 17). He is not speaking coldly or with relish; he loves the people who are rejecting his message and his God.

The final question in verse 27 contains a seed of hope: God's people will not be unclean forever. Jesus died for us to bear our shame and wash us clean, so that we can once again be God's people for God's renown and praise and honour. **Read 1 Corinthians 6:11 and Titus 3:3-7.**

⌄ Apply

The New Testament church has the same role: we are bound closely to God by being united to Christ, and we are meant to make his beauty visible in our lives. This is an honourable purpose! But if we are too proud to listen to his word, we are also useless for that purpose.

❓ *In what ways are you and your church listening to God's word and living in ways that honour Jesus?*

❓ *In what ways might you not be listening to God's word and therefore living in a way that dishonours Jesus?*

⌃ Pray

Praise God that he has bound us to himself and wants to use us to display his beauty to the world. Pray that you and your church would bring him renown and praise and honour.

When God won't answer

What happens next runs counter to our expectations: Jeremiah wants to pray for people more, and God tells him not to!

Israel is suffering a severe drought.

Read Jeremiah 14:1-9

- ❓ *What is there none of in Israel (v 2-6)?*
- ❓ *How does Jeremiah pray for the people (v 7-9)?*

Jeremiah is fulfilling his role as a prophet—praying for people in need.

Read Jeremiah 14:10-16

- ❓ *How does God respond to Jeremiah's prayer (v 10-12)?*
- ❓ *How come the other prophets have a much more positive message than Jeremiah (v 13-16)?*

The people have treated God like a genie who should grant their wishes, or a fairy godmother who should step in to solve all their problems. But that's not how relationships work—certainly not covenant relationships. If people continue to refuse to live God's way, there comes a point when it is too late to pray.

Jeremiah may have been told by God not to pray, but he can't help himself...

Read Jeremiah 14:17-22

- ❓ *What does God say will happen to his people (v 17-18)?*
- ❓ *What does Jeremiah say on their behalf (v 19-22)?*

This is a model prayer! How will God respond?

Read Jeremiah 15:1-9

- ❓ *How does God respond to Jeremiah's prayer (v 1-2)?*
- ❓ *What will happen to Jerusalem, that Jeremiah can no longer avert (v 3-9)?*

God's promise of blessing to Abraham was that his descendants would be more numerous than the sand of the sea (Genesis 22:17). Now that is reversed: the widows will be that numerous (Jeremiah 15:8).

▼ Apply

Prayer is not a magic technique for getting what we want; it is part of a relationship with God. If we constantly refuse to listen to God, then eventually he will, in effect, stop listening to us.

- ❓ *Do you seek God's direction as well as his salvation and his assistance?*
- ❓ *How can you ensure your prayers are about knowing God, not using him?*

One suggestion by way of answer to that question: use the Lord's prayer as the basis for your own prayers. That way, you will start with his glory and his will for your life, and not your needs.

▲ Pray

Spend some time in prayer now, responding to what has challenged you about prayer in this study.

Desperate times

When I am in a desperate situation, I become blind to everything else and my prayers become dominated by my need for help. We see a healthier pattern of prayer here.

Guard and guide me

Read Psalm 25:1-3

❓ *What does David ask for, and what confidence does he express?*

Read Psalm 25:4-5 and 8-9

Verses 8-9 show this is not a request for God to send him messages about which job to take, but that God would help him obey his word.

Be gracious to me

Read Psalm 25:6-7

God knows everything…

❓ *So why might David ask God to remember some things and forget others?*

It's a way of saying, "God, there are two undeniable realities: I am sinful and you are loving. When you are deciding whether to accept me, please bear in mind your love, not my sin." He's using "remember" in the way a teenager does when they say, "Remember how you promised you would give me driving lessons?" It's a plea to God to act on the basis of what he has said.

❓ *What does the phrase "sins of my youth" bring to mind as you look back on life?*

I don't think David mentions them because these sins are worse than the sins of old age. Rather, it is probably just that the sins of youth are more red-blooded and obvious, so they loom larger in David's conscience.

Faithful to bless

Read Psalm 25:8-15

❓ *What blessings of being God's people does David celebrate here?*

❓ *How would believing these truths affect how we pray and respond to difficulties?*

❓ *No one keeps the law of Moses perfectly, so what is David's only hope (v 11)?*

Help me!

Read Psalm 25:16-22

Finally we get to what has driven David to his knees in prayer. I love these verses. Isn't it wonderful that we have a God who cares about not just our eternal salvation, but also "the troubles of my heart"?

Is David's problem enemies or sin? These verses seem confused. But then, so is life! Our problems are a mixture of things that have happened to us as well as our sins. E.g. a broken relationship is painful; and it is much more painful if my unfaithfulness or temper contributed to the breakdown.

❓ *Who does David pray for in the final verse? How is that a challenge to us in our praying when we face crises?*

🔼 Pray

Use this psalm to help you pray either for yourself or (if life is not difficult for you right now) another Christian you know.

When God won't satisfy

Jeremiah's prayers are raw and honest. He doesn't hold back in telling God what he thinks of him. Here is another window into his turbulent prayer life.

Disillusioned

Read Jeremiah 15:10-14

❷ *How is Jeremiah feeling (v 10)?*

This isn't even really a prayer! Jeremiah seems to just be muttering to himself. Like Job, he even wishes he'd never been born.

God's response is in verses 11-14: verses 11-12 are spoken to Jeremiah, and verses 13-14 are spoken to the nation. On the one hand, Jeremiah will be protected and his message will be vindicated; on the other hand, the judgment will be terrible and life isn't going to get any easier for Jeremiah.

❷ *How reassuring would you say God's answer is?*

Dissatisfied

Jeremiah tries again.

Read Jeremiah 15:15-18

❷ *What does he say God is like (v 18)?*

In 2:13, God described himself as the spring of living water, the truly satisfying fountain. But Jeremiah isn't feeling it.

❷ *What do you make of Jeremiah's prayer here?*

❷ *What do you think it says about God that he inspired it to be in his Scriptures?*

Read Jeremiah 15:19-21

Sometimes God gives Jeremiah gentle reassurance; here, he dishes out a rebuke. He sees wounded pride in Jeremiah's words, an entitlement that thinks he deserves better.

❷ *What does he tell Jeremiah to do (v 19)?*

❷ *What does he promise if he does (v 19)?*

❷ *How does he reaffirm his commitment to Jeremiah from 1:18-19 (15:20-21)?*

⌄ Apply

It is understandable that someone going through what Jeremiah has might feel disillusionment, bitterness, resentment and self-pity. And that they might express these feelings in words. However, unchecked, these make us feel that God needs to repent, and others need to repent, but we don't.

Read Ephesians 4:31-32

❷ *Can you identify any disillusionment or bitterness or self-pity in yourself at the moment?*

❷ *If you can, how can you turn these into honest and worthy words in prayer? And how do you need to repent?*

⌃ Pray

Praise God that when we are filled with selfish resentment, he gently rebukes us and gives us beautiful promises like Jeremiah 15:20. Talk to God about any negative attitudes revealed by this passage, and ask for his help to repent where necessary.

Doom and gloom and hope

Jeremiah didn't just have to preach God's message of judgment. He had to bear the cost of embodying it in his life.

Isolation

Read Jeremiah 16:1-9

❓ *Why did God ban Jeremiah from...*
- *marrying and having children (v 1-4)?*
- *weeping with those who weep at funeral wakes (v 5-7)?*
- *rejoicing with those who rejoice at parties (v 8-9)?*

No family, no funerals, no feasts. This unusual life acted out God's message. It made people ask Jeremiah to give the reason for the hope he didn't have.

···· TIME OUT ·······································

❓ *God only gave these commands to Jeremiah. But in what ways do you think God's people today should be living differently, to show that we believe that a day of judgment will come?*

Consolation

Read Jeremiah 16:10-15

❓ *Why did God decree disaster (v 10-13)?*

❓ *What prospect could the Israelites look forward to on the other side of that judgment (v 14-15)?*

This is the prophetic pattern: judgment followed by salvation; exile followed by restoration; death followed by resurrection. This side of the first Easter, we can look back to an even greater redemption!

Read Jeremiah 16:16-21

❓ *What pictures does Jeremiah use to describe the judgment that is coming (v 16-18)?*

❓ *What will the nations do after that happens (v 19-21)?*

Jeremiah has been pleading for Israel to repent of their idolatry; in the future the nations will do just that! The majority of *Explore* readers are included in verse 19: Gentiles from the ends of the earth who've turned away from idols to know the Lord.

☑ Apply

Israel will be judged and exiled; then they will return; then after that the nations will turn to the Lord. This is the hope that consoled Jeremiah (v 19). The New Testament tells us this was fulfilled in Jesus, the true Israel: he was judged on Good Friday, returned at Easter, and since Pentecost the nations have been turning to him.

❓ *How does this hope console you when life and ministry are difficult—when embodying God's word is costly?*

↥ Pray

Praise Jesus, who fully bore the cost of embodying God's word in his life. Pray that God's global purposes would sustain you in sacrifices you make to live by faith and obey his word.

Heart searching

Heineken used to have an advert that claimed that it "refreshes the parts other beers can't reach". The same is true of God's salvation.

Engraved hearts

Read Jeremiah 17:1-4

❷ *What is written on people's hearts in Judah (v 1)?*

❷ *What will be the consequences (v 2-4)?*

God engraved the Ten Commandments on tablets of stone. Now Judah's sin is engraved on very different tablets. Their sin is set in concrete. In the Bible, the "heart" is like the engine of a car; it's the driving force in a person. If sin has gone that deep, what hope can there be?

Trusting heart

Read Jeremiah 17:5-8

❷ *What plant is someone like if they trust in man (v 5-6)?*

❷ *What about if they trust in God (v 7-8)?*

"I wish I had your faith," someone says. But we are all people of faith—the only difference is where we choose to put our trust. When we put our trust in the Lord, we will still experience heat and drought, but even then our fruit will be a blessing to others.

Tested heart

Read Jeremiah 17:9-13

❷ *What is God's verdict on our hearts (v 9)?*

❷ *How does verse 10 answer the question at the end of verse 9?*

Imagine hearing verse 9 as a prognosis for a physical disease: "You are beyond cure". How much worse that God should say that about our hearts! But there is hope.

Read Jeremiah 17:14

❷ *How is verse 14 the correct response to verse 9?*

If verses 14-18 show a prophet trusting God in practice, verses 19-27 show a city that doesn't.

⌄ Apply

Our hearts are beyond human cure, but God changes hearts.

Read Jeremiah 31:33-34

❷ *How has this chapter encouraged you to trust in the Lord rather than in yourself or other people?*

⌃ Pray

Put Jeremiah 17:14 in your own words, and pray it for yourself.

Then pray the Collect for Purity from the Anglican prayer book: "Almighty God, unto whom all hearts be open, all desires known, and from whom no secrets are hid: cleanse the thoughts of our hearts by the inspiration of thy Holy Spirit, that we may perfectly love thee, and worthily magnify thy holy Name; through Christ our Lord. Amen."

❤ *Bible in a year: 2 Kings 9 – 11 • 2 Chronicles 23*

Will God change the plan?

Is there any point in repenting? Does it make any difference how we respond to God's word if he has already announced what will happen?

A broken pot reshaped

Read Jeremiah 18:1-12

❓ *What did Jeremiah see at the potter's house (v 1-4)?*

❓ *How does God respond if:*
- *a nation facing his judgment turns back to him (v 5-8)?*
- *a nation promised his blessing turns away from him (v 9-10)?*

God rules the world with what the theologian Chris Wright calls a "responsive sovereignty". He is sovereign over nations like a potter is over his clay, but the clay can affect outcomes. But when God changes his actions, it is consistent with his character, his covenant and his purposes. When nations change their ways, God changes his plans for them. We do not believe in blind fate, but in a personal God.

❓ *How should the people of Judah respond to this knowledge (v 11)?*

❓ *But how do they respond instead (v 12)?*

Verses 13-23 show how the people were determined to continue with their own plans against Jeremiah and his God.

A broken pot not repaired

Read Jeremiah 19:1-13

❓ *What does God tell Jeremiah to do with a clay jar (v 1-2, 11)?*

❓ *What message does this symbolise (v 3, 11-13)?*

When clay is wet, it can be reshaped by the potter into a different type of jar (18:1-4). But once the clay has been hardened in the oven, it can't be repaired if it is broken (19:11). God is saying that Jerusalem has reached this hardened stage, the point of no return. Horrifyingly, those who sacrificed their children (v 5) will end up eating their children (v 9; compare Lamentations 4:10). That's why it is so urgent that we respond to God's warnings while we can.

⌄ Apply

Read James 4:8

❓ *How has Jeremiah 18 – 19 demonstrated...*
- *the opportunity to respond to God's warnings?*
- *the urgency of responding to God's warnings?*

❓ *Is the Holy Spirit convicting you of a particular sin at the moment and prompting you to repent of it? How will you respond?*

⌃ Pray

Praise God for the effectiveness of repentance—that he changes his stance towards us when we change our stance towards him. Pray that he would grant you a soft and repentant heart when you hear his word.

Bible in a year: 2 Chronicles 24 • Luke 21 • 2 Kings 12 – 13

Let down by God?

Have you ever felt that someone you trust has betrayed you? Can you remember the pain you felt? That's how Jeremiah feels towards God…

Read Jeremiah 19:14 – 20:6

❓ *What happened to Jeremiah after he preached the message of chapter 19?*

For the first time, Jeremiah experiences the physical suffering that God warned him about in 1:19. It produces his most passionate prayer.

Confused

Read Jeremiah 20:7-10

❓ *What does Jeremiah accuse God of (v 7)?*

❓ *What happens when Jeremiah does speak God's words (v 8)?*

❓ *What happens when he doesn't (v 9)?*

Jeremiah can't win. He wishes he didn't have such a negative, unpopular message. Serving God is harder than he'd expected, God hasn't protected him, no one listens, and his warnings haven't come true. Yet although he feels that God is his problem, he still prays, entrusting his problems to God.

Confident

Read Jeremiah 20:11-13

❓ *What does Jeremiah remember (v 11)?*

❓ *What does he pray for (v 12)?*

❓ *What does he praise God for (v 13)?*

As in chapter 11, Jeremiah both speaks to God about his feelings, and to his feelings about God. Is he over his wobble?

Cursed

Read Jeremiah 20:14-18

Verses 11-13 expressed the theology in Jeremiah's head; verses 14-18 express the pain that is still in his heart.

❓ *What is Jeremiah wishing for here?*

❓ *How does Jeremiah's prayer make you feel?*

Read Hebrews 5:7-10

❓ *In what ways is Jesus like Jeremiah (v 7)?*

❓ *Are there lines in Jeremiah's prayer that Jesus, as the obedient Son, would not have said?*

Jeremiah 20 and Hebrews 5:7 show how difficult it can be to live as God's servant and spokesperson. But whereas Jeremiah wanted to lose his life to avoid his mission, Jesus wanted to lose his life to fulfil his mission for us.

❓ *How does this move you to worship Jesus?*

⌄ Apply

❓ *How has Jeremiah 20 challenged your expectations of what it is like to serve God?*

❓ *If (or when next) you feel God has let you down, what can you learn from Jeremiah and Jesus about how to process your pain in prayer?*

If God is against us

Chapter 20 began with God saying judgment through the Babylonians was inevitable. In chapter 21, they arrive at the gates.

Read Jeremiah 21:1-2

(Note: this is a different Passhur to the one in chapter 20.)

- ❷ *What is the situation?*
- ❷ *What are Jerusalem's leaders hoping the Lord will do?*

They provoke God with their idolatry and injustice but still expect him to be at their beck and call. What will God say?

Tell King Zedekiah

The date is now 588 BC. Ten years before, the king of Babylon had installed Zedekiah as a puppet king: but then he had rebelled.

Read Jeremiah 21:3-7

- ❷ *God says "I will" 4 times. What is he about to do?*

Nebuchadnezzar is the least of their problems: God himself is now their enemy. And if God is against us, who can be for us?

···· TIME OUT ···

Read Deuteronomy 4:34; 7:1-2, 18-19

These verses describe what God was going to do to the evil Canaanites.

- ❷ *What links can you see between these verses and Jeremiah 21:3-7?*

God's people have been living and worshipping and sinning like Canaanites, so now God is going to treat them like Canaanites.

Tell the people

Read Jeremiah 21:8-10

The question has been "Will Israel repent?" Now that the Babylonians have arrived, it's "How should they respond to judgment?"

- ❷ *What action will lead to death?*
- ❷ *What action will lead to life?*

This sounds treacherous. Imagine a preacher telling Churchill and the British to surrender to Hitler, or Zelensky and the Ukrainians to surrender to Putin. But since the Babylonians were sent by God, that's what it looked like to submit to his rule.

Tell the royal family

Read Jeremiah 21:11-14

- ❷ *What is the first duty of rulers (v 11)?*
- ❷ *What picture does God use to describe his wrath (v 12, 14)?*

On this cliffhanger, we will now leave Jeremiah, and rejoin him in the next issue...

⌄ Apply

Read Hebrews 12:28-29

We are not in the same unique situation as Jerusalem in 588 BC, but our God is still a consuming fire.

- ❷ *How does this verse tell us to respond?*
- ❷ *What will that look like for you this week?*

Bible in a year: Jonah 1, Jonah 3 – 4 • Luke 8 ❤

Hollow words

"The Apprentice" on TV starts with boasts from the contestants who hope to be taken on, followed by an embarrassing display of the gap between their claims and abilities.

Read through Psalm 26 as if you are saying it to God, and then spend a minute or two thinking about whether your life matches up to the claims of the psalm.

Read Psalm 26

Oh dear. So how then should we pray this psalm? There are two things that help us work out what to do with it.

First, "blameless" doesn't always mean sinless in the Bible. Read Psalm 19:13. Here it means living a life that is not characterised by "wilful" sins—that is, sins that I happily indulge, rather than struggle and fight against. "Blameless" seems to be shorthand for "Lord, I may not be perfect, but I am a real believer, and you can see that from the way I live and the way I seek to live". After all, David asks God for mercy in 26:11, which he would not need if he was perfect. Similarly, the New Testament requires that church elders "must be blameless" (1 Timothy 3:2, NKJV). This can't mean sinless, or there would be no elders—and the remainder of the chapter shows that it means that they are to be leading an obviously Christian life. Psalm 26 is not about sinless perfection, but sincere devotion.

Second, even with that caveat we feel uncomfortable praying this psalm, and rightly so. The Bible encourages us to put our trust wholly in God's mercy, not our good deeds (Ephesians 2:8-9). There is only one man who could pray this psalm perfectly. There

is only one man who could ask God to vindicate him on the basis of his righteous life: Jesus.

With that in mind, look back through the psalm to see exactly what it says before we try to apply and pray it:

Read Psalm 26:1-3: *Examine me, O God, and you will find I trust and obey you!*

Read Psalm 26:4-5: *I do not allow ungodly voices to influence my behaviour.*

Read Psalm 26:6-8: *I am committed to deepening my relationship with you at church and to telling others about you.*

Read Psalm 26:9-12: *I have lived a blameless life, surrounded by wilful sinners—so please deliver me.*

▲ Pray

First, read slowly through the psalm, reflecting on the ways in which you fall short of these standards and confessing these to God.

Next, read slowly through the psalm, thinking how the Gospel accounts portray Jesus living out the life of this psalm, and praising him for this.

Finally, read slowly through Psalm 26, asking God to help you live more like Jesus in these areas of life.

2 THESSALONIANS: Worthy

Paul begins his second letter to the Thessalonian church with rejoicing.

Read 2 Thessalonians 1:1-5

Pray

Paul twice calls God "our Father" in verses 1-2. (Although the NIV has "*the* Father" in verse 2, the Greek reads "our".) He is asking his readers to ponder their relationship with God!

Re-read verses 1-2 out loud, slowly.

- ❷ *Why does it matter to you today that God is your Father?*
- ❷ *In what ways do you need his grace and peace?*

Growing and increasing

- ❷ *Which words in verse 3 emphasise how important it is to give thanks?*
- ❷ *Why do you think it's helpful to start with thanksgiving?*
- ❷ *What are you thankful for today?*

Paul is thankful for the evidence of God's grace in the lives of these believers. They are growing in faith, increasing in love and persevering through trials.

Paul's priorities are shown in what he is most thankful for. They have faith and love, and he knows that this is the most important thing for them. It's a helpful pointer to what we ought to be thankful for—and to what we ought to prioritise in the lives of those we love.

- ❷ *How might the Thessalonian believers' faith and love help them to persevere in suffering?*
- ❷ *How might their suffering help them to grow in faith and love?*
- ❷ *What does their faith, love and perseverance prove about them (v 5)?*

We tend to think we should avoid suffering at all costs. But in the first generation of Christianity, it was seen as a privilege—a way God refined his people.

Counted worthy

Read 2 Thessalonians 1:11-12

We'll look at verses 6-10 in the next study.

- ❷ *What's the ultimate goal of growing in godliness (v 12)?*
- ❷ *How does growing in faith and goodness work (v 11)? What is God's role? What role do we play?*
- ❷ *In summary, how do we become "worthy of [God's] calling"?*

Pray

Take some time to reflect.

- ❷ *What do you want to give thanks for as a result of what you've read?*
- ❷ *Who could you pray for using the words of Paul's prayer?*

A God of justice

Why would God allow the Thessalonians to endure trials? We've had part of an answer—now here's some more.

Read 2 Thessalonians 1:5-10

It may seem strange to say that suffering is evidence of God's justice. If God is sovereign and good, why would his people be suffering simply for believing in him? Yet Paul insists that God's righteous judgment is demonstrated—not disproved—by what the Thessalonian believers are going through. How?

First, Paul is saying that God is just in regard to the Thessalonians. He is working through their suffering to make them grow in faith. So, on the day of judgment, it will clearly be just that they are counted worthy of God's kingdom, because of their godliness.

Second, Paul is saying that God is just in punishing the unjust. People who cause the righteous to suffer should be punished—and God will punish them.

True wrongdoing

Persecuting the Thessalonian church is not the only—and not the worst—crime committed by these wrongdoers. They are also those who "do not know God and do not obey the gospel of our Lord Jesus". Whereas Paul commends the Christians for believing his testimony, these afflicters have rejected it. They have heard the good news and chosen to ignore it and disobey God. This carries eternal consequences.

❓ What will those who have rejected Jesus be shut out from (v 9)? Why is this more evidence of God's justice?

❓ How else does Paul describe the future day of God's judgment? What will happen?

❓ What will it be like for those who believe?

Paul says that God will grant relief to those who have been afflicted (v 7). This relief is not only an end to suffering but the joy of seeing the Lord Jesus revealed.

Pray

❓ Who do you know who is suffering at the moment?

❓ What Christian communities around the world do you know of that are facing persecution?

Pray for them now in light of what you've read. Cry out to God for justice and relief—both now and in eternity. Ask for God's comfort in distress for these suffering believers.

❓ Who do you know who is currently in a state of having rejected Jesus?

Pray for them too. Ask God to change their hearts so that they can ultimately come into his presence and experience his goodness.

The man of lawlessness

Get ready for one of the most difficult-to-interpret passages in the New Testament...

No small amount of ink has been spilt over the last 2,000 years by commentators attempting to explain exactly what Paul is talking about here! But don't be worried. God has something important to tell us through these words.

Read 2 Thessalonians 2:1-4

Paul's purpose

❷ *What is Paul writing about (v 1)?*

❷ *What lie have the Thessalonian believers heard (v 2)?*

❷ *What is Paul's intention and hope for his readers (v 2)?*

This passage teaches us that it is not a bad thing to wrestle with questions or voice your doubts. We must be brothers and sisters who wrestle with hard questions together. Equally, it is a bad thing to only question things and never reach for, or accept, answers. We don't need to stay unsettled! God has truth for us to help us when we are confused or afraid.

❷ *What's the clear truth Paul delivers in verse 3, to help his readers be confident?*

The man of lawlessness

Paul's basic message is clear. You don't need to be worried you've missed the day of the Lord, because something obvious will happen before that day comes.

But what—or who—exactly is Paul describing?

People throughout history have tried to identify one of their own contemporaries as this "man of lawlessness". One of the Roman emperors? A corrupt pope? It goes on and on. But let's go back to what Paul spells out for us about this figure.

- He is the "man of lawlessness". He is against the law. He rebels against God and man.

- He is doomed to destruction. He will lose. He will not win against God.

- He will set himself up in the place of God.

That's what we know about this "man of sin". He will work against God, but he will never defeat or disrupt God's plans.

Paul's purpose in saying these things is not to help us to identify exactly who this figure is. It's to warn us: Don't be deceived. When he comes and he makes his claims, don't you be deceived; make sure you are ready.

⌄ Apply

❷ *When doubts shake you, what can you do to help yourself focus on God's truth?*

❷ *Why is it especially important as we look to the future to remember that God is sovereign and his plans will not fail?*

How to not be deceived

The man of lawlessness might seem mysterious, but we have all we need to avoid being deceived by him.

Read 2 Thessalonians 2:5-12

Our defence

Paul has not left the Thessalonians un-armed against this spiritual deception. He has already taught them the word of God (1 Thessalonians 2:13). They just need to remember what they have learned (2 Thessalonians 2:5). It is no different for us. If we are to avoid being taken in by any kind of false teaching, we need to know, remember, and stand on the true word of God.

The Scriptures don't tell us every detail about the end times, but they do tell us enough. As we've already seen, the key point is that God is in sovereign control. We need to trust in Christ to deliver us safely through.

⌄ Apply

❷ *How secure do you feel in your knowledge of God's word?*

❷ *What is one step you could take to grow in knowledge of God's word?*

The restrainer

Who is "the one who now holds it back" in verse 7? Many commentators think this restraining force is the presence of government, which restrains lawlessness and persecution. But we can't arrive at certainty on this question.

But the identity of this figure isn't Paul's main point. The main point is that God is in control.

❷ *In what ways do we see that through verses 7-12?*

Satan's playbook

Verses 9-10 tell us that the man of lawless-ness will work just like Satan: through lies. Satan causes people to misjudge God and worship something else instead (see Genesis 3:1-5; Romans 1:25). God's response to this is to give people over to their choice—in the language of 2 Thessalonians 2:11, to send them a strong delusion so that they keep believing what they have chosen to believe.

This doesn't just apply to the end times; it applies to us, any time we're tempted to idolise anything other than the true God. But we have an advantage: we know Satan's strategy. Paul wants to prepare us for the deception of the evil one so that we will stand firm.

⌃ Pray

❷ *In what ways are you tempted to idolise human success or to prioritise wealth, health, or prosperity? Or to prioritise anything else that is not God?*

Take some time to ask for God's help to live in the light of the truth about him instead.

Truths to stand on

The hymn "Amazing Grace" by John Newton warns us that every Christian will go through dangers, toils and snares. But there's something that brings us through.

It's God's grace!

Read 2 Thessalonians 2:13-14

❷ *What has God done to bring the Thessalonians through thus far?*

❷ *And how will he bring them through in the future?*

Four truths

There are four truths to cling to in these verses. See if you can spot each one in the passage.

- *God loves his people.* Paul wants these believers to relish the reality of God's love for them.
- *God chose his people to be saved.* The best translation of the phrase in verse 13 is actually "chose you from the beginning". Before the world was, God chose us! That means that his love for us doesn't depend on our own efforts. It depends on the unchanging God, and we can find deep assurance in that.
- *God sanctifies his people by his Spirit.* This is one sense in which our salvation is on-going. We are being refined and prepared for the place of righteousness where we will one day make our home. We do play a role in this ourselves, but most importantly, the Holy Spirit is working through us to grow in godliness.
- *God calls his people.* Our future is one in which we will obtain the glory of the Lord

Jesus Christ. We might not feel glorious now, but we are waiting for a glorious inheritance!

🔼 Pray

❷ *Who do you know who might particularly need to know that they are loved by God at the moment?*

❷ *Who do you know who needs assurance that they are really saved?*

❷ *In what ways do you see God sanctifying people around you?*

❷ *Is there anyone you know who you long to see grow in Christian maturity, or who feels stuck in sinfulness?*

❷ *Who do you know who might feel particularly non-glorious at the moment?*

Take some time to lift each of these individuals to the Lord in prayer.

Then read through verses 13-14 again and meditate on these amazing truths for yourself. Praise God for his work in you and ask him to help you find comfort in it.

You might like to listen to the hymn "Amazing Grace" to help you continue to praise God.

Clinging on

In 1987 Henry Dempsey, a commercial pilot, was flying a small plane from Boston, Massachusetts to Lewiston, Maine, when he heard a strange rattle.

Dempsey left his co-pilot to fly the plane, and went to find out what it was. But the door at the back of the plane opened unexpectedly and he fell out. He grabbed onto the railing of the boarding steps and hung on for his life—4,000 feet above the Atlantic Ocean!

When the plane landed and the emergency services reached Dempsey, he was still holding on so tight that they had to peel his hands free from the railing.

That's how hard we need to cling to the truth about God!

Read 2 Thessalonians 2:15-17

❓ *What difference did it make to you yesterday to meditate on the truths in verses 13-14?*

❓ *What difference do you think it can continue to make to cling to these truths—perhaps to the way you act, the way you see yourself, the way you think about the future, or your relationship with God in general?*

Eternal encouragement

Verses 16-17 must have been a beautiful thing to read for the Thessalonian believers. It represents Paul's deep aspiration—his profound desire for blessing from God for his Thessalonian brothers and sisters.

︿ Pray

Read through the blessing slowly before you go on. Pay attention to the words. Imagine Paul is praying it for you! Then add your own prayers to God.

···· TIME OUT ··························

It's significant that Paul mentions Jesus' name before the Father's. Paul was once a Pharisee, and he took the Old Testament Scriptures extremely seriously! He believed that there is only one God, and we should have no other gods before him. So, the phrasing here represents Paul's belief that Jesus is fully divine—and that Father, Son, and Spirit are distinct, but are one God. To prove the point, Paul then switches to the singular for "who loved … and … gave", emphasising the unity of Christ and the Father.

Blessing in practice

Notice that Paul prays for God to establish his readers in "every good deed and word". The Christian life isn't just sitting around and contemplating the blessings that the Lord has given us. It is living out of those blessings! Paul wants every word and work of ours to glorify God—that's what we were created, and recreated in Christ, to do.

Of course, we need help with that! And that's precisely why Paul is asking God for blessing.

From warfare to worship

What do you most want from God? Here David is, once again, in mortal danger. What does he most want from God? Not God's protection and deliverance, but God himself.

The Messiah had to…

Read Luke 24:26-27

> ❷ What did the Messiah have to do, does Jesus tell these two followers?

Jesus then took them through the Old Testament to prove it. Where did he go? Isaiah 53 is one place where we see God's servant afflicted and killed, but where else? This is where David and the psalms are crucial. David was the Lord's anointed king, the shadow of the one to come—Jesus. David's psalms are dominated by his rejection, his enemies and his suffering. Since David's experience tells us what to expect from the life of his greater descendant, then it's clear that the Christ—the Messiah—had to suffer before entering his glory.

Surrounded but secure

Read Psalm 27:1-3

> ❷ What dangers does David face here?
> ❷ Why is he not afraid? How does he describe God?

Captivated by beauty

Read Psalm 27:4-6

The warfare stops, the guns fall silent and suddenly the warrior is a worshipper. The language is poetic and we should avoid being over-literal in how we interpret it.

> ❷ Having said that, what feelings about God is David expressing?
> ❷ Why does David want to be near God?

Show your face

Read Psalm 27:7-12

David knows that God is his only hope and so he prays to him for help. To turn your face towards someone is to give them your attention, to be open to them and personally concerned for them.

> ❷ What else does David pray for (v 11-12)?

Wait for the Lord

Read Psalm 27:13-14

> ❷ What does David believe about God in these last two verses, and what does it lead him to do?

Waiting for the Lord (v 14) is not vain hope. It is a bold declaration of faith; a refusal to stop believing God is good when circumstances suggest God has forgotten you. For many of us this is where the spiritual battle in our own lives will be fiercest. In our darkest hour will we abandon faith in God, or will we, like David, "wait for the LORD"?

⌄ Apply

> ❷ Is there a way you need to "wait" at the moment? How does this psalm help you do that?

Confident prayers

When you pray with others, what would you say the tone of your prayers is? Joyful? Concerned? Pleading? Despairing?

In 2 Thessalonians 3, Paul shows us what it looks like to pray with great confidence.

Read 2 Thessalonians 3:1-5

❓ *Where do we see Paul's confidence in these verses?*

❓ *What is his confidence based on?*

Paul's requests

❓ *What does Paul ask for prayer for in verses 1-2?*

Paul's language in verse 1 comes right out of the psalms: "He sends his command to the earth; his word runs swiftly" (Psalm 147:15). It's a prayer for the spread and the success of the gospel. If you ever wonder how to pray for church leaders, evangelists, missionaries, church-planters, or preachers, this would be a great prayer! The faithfulness and abilities of human ministers are not what brings success. We need God's blessing.

Paul is confident to ask this because God's word has already run swiftly among the Thessalonians. God has already started this work! And the Thessalonians ought to be particularly excited to be part of the spread of the gospel through their prayers.

❓ *In what ways has God been at work in your life in the past?*

❓ *How could you turn those experiences into prayers for others?*

❓ *Who might God be calling you to persevere in prayer for?*

Paul's second request is not theoretical. He was constantly being opposed by people who contradicted the gospel. In our own day, we will need to pray this prayer more and more, since hindering the gospel is now more possible and more common in the Western world than it has been for a long time.

❓ *Where have you seen or heard about people opposing or trying to hinder the gospel?*

Factoring in reality

❓ *When might you lack confidence in your prayers? What do you think the cause of that might be?*

When we think of the opposition we face, it can be daunting. The world, the flesh, and the devil are all arrayed against us! Yet we are in a battle that only the Lord can win. He has said, "I will not forsake you". So why are we afraid? Paul is right: we can have confidence that God is at work. We simply need to continue to pray for perseverance and faith.

Pray

Consider the situations and individuals you have thought about in this study so far. Use the words of verse 5 to pray for them, and for yourself, now.

A model to imitate

In his first letter to the Thessalonians, Paul told them to "warn those who are idle and disruptive" (1 Thessalonians 5:14).

There were some people in the Thessalonian church who were expecting Jesus to return immediately, and so they quit work and depended upon the benevolence of other (still working) Christians to take care of them. Paul told them to keep working! But this problem had not gone away.

Read 2 Thessalonians 3:6-10

❓ *What was Paul's original teaching about this (v 10)?*

❓ *How did he live up to that teaching himself (v 7-9)?*

Don't be lazy

Why is idleness such a problem? Paul's own example reveals the answer. Although the normal pattern was for congregations to support their pastor, Paul worked so that he could support himself (see 1 Timothy 5:17-18 and 1 Corinthians 9:3-7, 14). He did not want to unnecessarily burden the people he was ministering to. The same reasoning applies to all of us.

❓ *Why could not working create unnecessary burdens on others?*

❓ *In what situations is not working actually a good and necessary thing?*

The Scriptures also show us that work is glorious. God designed humans to work (see Genesis 1:27; 2:15) and he tells us that our work is a way of serving him, even if it seems like we are just serving other humans (Colossians 3:23-24).

Paul expects the word of God to be obeyed. Idleness might not seem that serious to us, but for Paul it means turning away from God's teaching. This is a major problem!

⌄ Apply

Think about your own work. This could include unpaid work.

❓ *What does your work provide for you? What are you grateful for in it?*

❓ *How does your toil serve others? How do you think it could bring glory to God?*

❓ *Why is Paul a good model to imitate? How could you follow his example in your own work?*

Keep away

We'll think more about Paul's instruction to keep away from idle believers in the next study.

❓ *For now, why do you think this might be a helpful instruction for the faithful believers?*

❓ *What might the impact be on the idle believers?*

⌃ Pray

Thank God for your work, and ask for his wisdom to labour well for his glory.

Busy, not busybodies

In today's passage, Paul reveals that at the heart of his instructions about idleness is a concern that the Thessalonian church will thrive.

Read 2 Thessalonians 3:11-15

❓ *The idle believers are not just not working—what do they seem to be doing instead (v 11)?*

Verse 13 suggests that the congregation has become discouraged by this minority of idle busybodies. They're frustrated. They've had enough! But Paul urges them not to stop doing the right thing.

When some in a church are not living in accord with the Bible, it can be discouraging and frustrating. It sows the thought, "Why bother?" But Paul doesn't want us to be distracted by that voice. He wants us to continue to pursue holiness.

Do not condone

❓ *How should the faithful believers treat the idle believers (v 14-15)?*

❓ *Why?*

We all need to play an active part in mutual accountability in our local church. It needs to be clear that sin is not accepted. Why? Because it's serious! We need to call each other to live like Christians. Lovingly confronting another person about their sin can be hard, but it can bring people back from acting in a way that is out of accord with God's word. These are family members, not enemies—and we need to win them back.

❓ *How would you sum up Paul's instructions in verses 6-15?*

❓ *What would it look like in your church to put these things into practice?*

The Lord of peace

Read 2 Thessalonians 3:16-18

Paul's final benediction reminds us that only the Lord can give us real peace—and that he is able to give it to us at all times, in all ways, in all places, and in all circumstances.

The Thessalonians needed peace not only within themselves but also between themselves. The letter of 2 Thessalonians shows that there was worry and division among them. They needed unity, and that can only come from the Lord of peace—the one who died on the cross for all his people. We cannot look down on brothers and sisters when we are on our knees together before the throne of grace.

It is as the Thessalonians all grow together in their experience and enjoyment of the grace, peace and presence of the Lord Jesus Christ that they will hold fast to the truth and walk with endurance in their trials, until the day the Lord Jesus returns.

🔼 Pray

Turn what you have read into praise for the Lord Jesus and prayers for your own church family.

DANIEL: Faithful in exile

Welcome to Daniel. It's around 605 BC and God's people are living in exile away from God's land, in the heart of a powerful and prosperous pagan empire: Babylon.

But why? What went so wrong that the Israelites would end up here?

Read Daniel 1:1-2

❷ *Look at where Nebuchadnezzar puts the articles from the temple of God (v 2). What answer would he give to the question "why", do you think?*

❷ *Look at the crucial detail we get at the start of verse 2. How does that explain what is really going on?*

···· TIME OUT ···································

2 Kings 24 – 25 describes a series of invasions by the Babylonian King Nebuchadnezzar during the reigns of three kings of Judah, of which Jehoiakim is the first. Each defeat proves worse than the one before, until Jerusalem is finally overthrown (around 20 years after Daniel 1:1).

❷ *Read 2 Kings 24:1-4. How does this answer the question, "why"?*

Meet the cast

Read Daniel 1:3-7

❷ *In what sense is this a good gig for Daniel & Co?*

❷ *What are the (serious) downsides?*

If Israel's god is the one true God, then right now it really doesn't look like it. His treasures are in the storehouses of the Babylonian gods. His people have lost the land he gave them and the freedom he won for them. And now they're compelled to live and work in Babylon.

They even lose their names (v 7). Daniel's Hebrew name means "God is my judge". But his new name Belteshazzar declares that "Bel (a Babylonian god) protects my life". Similarly, Azariah ("he the Lord helps") becomes Abednego ("servant of Nebo", another Babylonian deity). Israel has lost—and their God has lost too. Or so it seems...

But as this book develops, the truth of God's sovereignty over all things, that is stated so simply in verse 2, will be dramatically revealed and illustrated through miraculous rescues, reversals of fortune, and terrifying visions of the future. The lives of rulers and nations, and every individual within them, are in the Lord's hands.

Daniel was probably written fairly soon after the end of exile (in around 539 BC). But life wasn't easy for those who returned to the land—in many ways it still looked like they were the losers. The book of Daniel was intended to help them to learn the lessons of the past, and to stay faithful in the future as they rebuilt Jerusalem.

⌃ Pray

When do you think it looks as if God is "losing"? Talk to God about it now. Rejoice that however it looks, God is not losing. Pray that reading Daniel will increase your confidence in his loving, fatherly rule.

Going vegan

Yesterday we met four teenagers from among the Israelite captives: Daniel, Hananiah, Mishael and Azariah.

Fortunately for them, they're not stuck making bricks on a Babylonian building project. Instead, they've been put on a cushy cultural training programme, complete with lavish rations from the king's table. Cue a plot twist that hinges on a three-letter word ... *but*.

Read Daniel 1:8-17

❓ *What does Daniel "resolve" in verse 8? What does he do about it (v 9, 11-14)?*

❓ *What does God do for Daniel (v 9, 17)?*

What was it about the king's food and drink that would have "defiled" Daniel? We can't be sure. It's possible that it was because it would have violated the food laws laid down in Leviticus (e.g. Leviticus 3:17; 11:47), or because it was sacrificed to pagan gods.

Whatever the reason, it's clear that Daniel's priority isn't keeping his head down for an easy life. Nor is it maximising the "strategic" opportunities of being trained for the Babylonian court. His priority is staying faithful to his God. And his resolve is firm: when the chief official proves sympathetic but reluctant (Daniel 1:9-10), Daniel finds another way (v 11-13).

Highs and lows

Three years of vegetables later (see v 5)...

Read Daniel 1:18-21

❓ *How does the writer emphasise the exceptional abilities of these young men (v 19-20)? What's their secret (v 17)?*

These four young captives are honoured as the best in the business. This is a pattern we'll see a lot of in Daniel: the low are raised up, and the high are brought low.

⬇ Apply

❓ *Do you share Daniel's resolve to live a life of counter-cultural obedience and purity? In what specific areas does your resolve feel weak?*

❓ *What elements of your environment/ circumstances pose a threat to your resolve?*

Two phrases in Daniel 1 will sharpen our resolve: "God had caused..." (v 9), "God gave..." (v 17). God equips us for obedience, and he rewards our obedience. He works in our circumstances to always provide a way out of temptation (1 Corinthians 10:13); and he gives us his Spirit to empower us to say "no" to temptation (Galatians 5:16-26). And he promises that living his way will *always* result in blessing, either in this life or the next (Luke 11:28; 12:35-38). (Although that doesn't mean everything will always go well with us, as we'll see in Daniel chapter 3.)

❓ *God has promised to equip us and reward us for our obedience. How does this spur you on to live a holy life?*

Prayers in a crisis

How do you respond in a crisis? This passage invites us to compare how two very different men react under pressure.

It's worth noting that 2:4 – 7:28 are written in Aramaic (the most universally understood language of the ancient world) as opposed to Hebrew. These central chapters contain a message that is for all nations.

Read Daniel 2:1-13

❓ *Why is this king—the most powerful man in the ancient world—so troubled?*

❓ *Look at the way the writer has chosen to describe this back-and-forth dialogue between the king and his astrologers.*
• What words and ideas are repeated?
• How does the way the story is told keep raising the tension?

❓ *What have the astrologers got right in their frustrated outburst in verses 10-11?*

❓ *How would you describe the king's response in verses 12-13?*

Read Daniel 2:14-19

❓ *How would you describe Daniel's response in these verses?*

❓ *How does that compare with Nebuchadnezzar's?*

We've already been told in 1:17 that Daniel has the God-given ability to interpret dreams and visions. So when he hears about the drama in the palace, he acts *prudently* (in his delicate words to Arioch), *confidently* (in approaching the king), *humbly* (in seeking the help of others), and *prayerfully* (in pleading for mercy from God). It's clear that those things are not mutually exclusive!

⌄ Apply

Think about a time recently when you were facing either a crisis, something unknown or had just received bad news.

❓ *Which of those four marks of Daniel's response could have been said of your reaction (prudent, confident, humble, prayerful)? Which less so?*

❓ *How might a more Daniel-like response have looked?*

"There is no one on earth who can do what the king asks" (v 10). But there is a God in heaven who can. "The gods ... do not live among humans" (v 11). But our God does. The Babylonian gods may have been distant, but the Lord is at work in his world—revealing himself, speaking to his people, and showing mercy. He did this ultimately by becoming human: "He has spoken to us by his Son ... [who is] the radiance of God's glory and the exact representation of his being" (Hebrews 1:2-3). We don't need to panic or grope in the darkness. God has made himself known. If, like Daniel, we know we have a God in heaven who is at work in the world, then this will lead us to pray, and to act with prayerful confidence.

⌃ Pray

You have a God in heaven who is at work in the world. What do you need to talk to him about today?

Credit-card prayers

Credit cards enable you to buy something you can't pay for now, on the basis that you promise to pay for it later. It's easy to pray "credit-card prayers".

Here's how they sound: "God, if you'll only get me out of this mess I've made, I promise that I'll go to church regularly / tell my family about Jesus / (Insert promise here)."

There's nothing wrong with promising to do things for God—but that's not how to pray to God, as we see in this psalm.

Cry for mercy

Read Psalm 28:1-2

David was a mighty warrior, a man of great personal bravery. But he is clear that unless God helps him, he is done for. "Down to the pit" is Bible language for death.

And David asks for "mercy"—undeserved kindness. David can't offer or promise anything to God to pay for his rescue. He has nothing to offer in return for God's help.

Cry for justice

Read Psalm 28:3-5

If God is going to have mercy on David, it will involve him dealing with David's enemies. So David also cries out for justice. This sort of prayer makes us very uncomfortable. It's worth recognising that it is not the only thing that the Bible has to say about how we relate to our enemies (see for example Luke 6:27-36). But these verses are also true and helpful.

❓ *What exactly does he ask God to do?*

This is not a cry for gratuitous torture and bloodthirsty revenge. It's a plea for justice.

❓ *How might these verses help a Christian refugee family fleeing from Syria?*

❓ *Or a wife who has been cheated on or abused by her husband?*

We do not need to take justice into our own hands because we know that God will one day do it (Romans 12:19). But we are right to pray for it.

Cry of praise

Read Psalm 28:6-9

❓ *When God has shown mercy to him, how does David respond (v 6-7)?*

❓ *What blessings do verses 8-9 show, which all God's people can enjoy?*

❓ *How do we benefit from God rescuing our King, his Son Jesus, from the grave?*

David can pray with confidence for mercy and justice from the same God. How the perfect Judge can show mercy is a tension that is unresolved at this point in the Bible, until it happens wondrously in the blood of the cross of Christ (Romans 3:25-26).

🔼 Pray

As you pray, remember to be conscious that you cannot earn God's help or forgiveness, or promise to pay for it later like a credit-card bill. Rely on the fact that he does these things for us because he is merciful.

Revelation and praise

Nebuchadnezzar wants his wise men to tell him his dream and interpret it. If Daniel doesn't come up with an answer soon, he'll be cut into pieces! No sweat…

Read Daniel 2:19-23

❓ *How does Daniel arrive at an understanding of the king's dream (v 19, 23)?*

❓ *What does he immediately do next (v 19)?*

Today we're going to hit pause on the narrative and spend some time praising God with Daniel. You might find it helpful to jot down your answers to the following questions on a piece of paper; then at the end of the study, you can turn your notes into your own song of praise. Optional New Testament references are listed to further stimulate your worship.

He changes

Read Daniel 2:21a; Romans 13:1

❓ *How have you seen the "times and seasons" change around you lately? God did it!*

❓ *Who is in authority over you? God put them there!*

He gives

Read Daniel 2:21b; James 1:5

❓ *Who do you admire for their wisdom and discernment? God gave it to them!*

He reveals

Read Daniel 2:22; 1 John 1:5-7

❓ *What dark thoughts are you ashamed of? God knows them!*

❓ *What dark or unknown things are you afraid of? God overrules them!*

Thanks and praise

Read Daniel 2:23; 1 John 5:14-15

God is the source and holder of all wisdom and power (Daniel 2:20); yet he freely gives wisdom and power to his servants (v 23).

❓ *What has God "made known" to you through his word in the last few weeks or months? Are there particular things he has been teaching you?*

❓ *List some specific ways in which God has given you "what [you] asked of him" in answer to your prayers.*

⌃ Pray

Read through verses 20-23 again, making them your own prayer of praise; at the end of each line, turn your answers to today's questions into words of worship and thanksgiving. Do this out loud if possible!

Bible in a year: Hosea 1 – 3 • Ezekiel 37 ⌄

Weird dreams

Ever had a weird dream that made you afraid? We're about to listen in on Nebuchadnezzar's…

Read Daniel 2:24-30

We'll return to these verses tomorrow. Today we will focus on the content of the dream itself, which reveals "what will happen in days to come". Try to really imagine what you're reading—draw some pictures if it helps!

Read Daniel 2:31-43

- **❷** *What's impressive about this statue (v 31)? What ultimately happens to it (v 34-35)?*
- **❷** *What is impressive about Nebuchadnezzar's kingdom (v 37-38)?*
- **❷** *What ultimately will happen to it (along with all the others that follow)?*

The four kingdoms represented by the four parts of the statue are generally accepted to be the Babylonian, Medo-Persian, Greek and Roman Empires. It's hard to underestimate the splendour of the Babylonian Empire at this stage of history. Nebuchadnezzar stands at the head of a kingdom that was both militarily dominant and culturally magnificent. And yet he is told that "after you...", someone else will come. His kingdom and those that follow will eventually be "swept ... away without leaving a trace" (v 35).

⌄ Apply

What are some of the things in the world around you that look powerful and permanent? There will be a time "after them". Just as there will be a time "after you". Whatever it is that you pour your effort into building: a career, a home, or even a ministry—one

day another person will sit at your desk, another family will live in your house, another person will lead your group. This truth should humble us. Even good things aren't permanent. Except, that is, for one...

The living stone

Read Daniel 2:44-45

- **❷** *In what ways is this final kingdom different to the others?*

Gold, bronze, iron or clay... it doesn't matter. There are really only two categories: things that will *end*, and the thing that will *endure* for ever—Christ's kingdom. There will never be a time "after him"; there will only and ever be him. These verses began to be fulfilled at the cross; and will be fully realised when Christ returns. He is the living Stone. And wonderfully, "the one who trusts in him will never be put to shame" or destroyed (1 Peter 2:4, 6). What we build on this foundation will endure (1 Corinthians 3:11-14).

⌄ Apply

- **❷** *What would change about what you do today, and how you do it, if you...*
  - *remembered that "after you" will come someone else?*
  - *remembered that what you do for Christ's kingdom will endure?*
- **❷** *How would that change the way you think about the rich/powerful/successful people you know?*

Bible in a year: Hosea 4 – 5, Hosea 7 – 8

Rise and fall...

Daniel has just told the most powerful man in the world that one day his kingdom will be destroyed, and succeeded by a kingdom set up by the "God of heaven" himself.

❓ *How do you think he'll respond?*

Before we find out, let's rewind the narrative to re-live the moments before the dream was revealed.

Mystery solved

Read Daniel 2:24-30, 46-49

❓ *Where did Daniel get the interpretation of the dream from (v 28, 30, 47)?*

❓ *Why has this mystery been revealed to Nebuchadnezzar (v 30)?*

❓ *How does this show God's kindness, do you think?*

❓ *How would you describe Nebuchadnezzar's response to this revelation?*

❓ *What is satisfying about how things end for Daniel and his friends?*

Clearly, the theme of God revealing mysteries is significant in this chapter. Look at how many times it comes up: verses 22, 28, 29, 30, 47!

And here's why this is important. The only way we can hope to know *anything* about who God is—or get answers to any of our big questions about who we are and why we're here and what the world is for—is if God tells us. If we were left to our own devices, we'd be scrabbling around in the dark: confused and afraid. But God speaks. He reveals mysteries; he reveals himself. He

gives a personal revelation to a pagan king. How kind; how glorious!

But in the New Testament, God goes one better. It's interesting that, in the Gospels, Jesus never receives or interprets dreams, when this is something we see so much of in the Old Testament. But this makes perfect sense: Jesus doesn't need to interpret God's revelation, because he *is* God's revelation. **Read Hebrews 1:1-3.** So, as New Testament believers, we stand in a position more privileged than Nebuchadnezzar or Daniel. Because we see much more than a dream of a rock; we see The Rock himself.

"No one has ever seen God, but the one and only Son ... has made him known" (John 1:18). God speaks in order to save—by his Son, through his word. Paul speaks of God's salvation plan of the cross as "God's wisdom, a mystery that has been hidden and that God destined for our glory before time began" (1 Corinthians 2:7). The world around us won't get it, but "these are the things God has revealed to us by his Spirit" (1 Corinthians 2:10).

🔼 Pray

Like Nebuchadnezzar, we should be flat on our faces in awe. Not praising the human messenger, but praising the "God of gods and the Lord of kings" who would reveal himself to us.

❓ *Why not do that now?*

Odd one out

Ever had the experience of trying to walk when a crowd is pushing past you the opposite way? Does your faith ever make you feel like the odd one out?

Read Daniel 3:1-7

❓ *What details are we given that show the super-sized scale of this event?*

The statue is around 27m tall (about the height of six double decker buses!)—probably an image of the Babylonian god Nebu, whom Nebuchadnezzar was named after. There's also an orchestra in attendance.

The king calls for his officials (v 2), and they come (v 3). He tells them to bow down on the signal (v 5), and they do (v 7). A crowd of "all ... nations" and "every language" fall on their faces and worship. Except for three...

Read Daniel 3:8-18

❓ *What might you want to reply to Nebuchadnezzar's question in verse 15?*

❓ *What do you find most striking about their reply in verses 16-18?*

⌄ Apply

Shadrach, Meshach and Abednego lived in a culture that put them under pressure—and so do we.

❓ *What are the "gods" (values/ideas/ things) that the people around you "worship" (pursue/esteem highly/ demand that others respect)? Think about areas of life where...*
  • *you get swept along with the crowd without noticing it.*
  • *your choices/views are questioned or "denounced" by others.*

  • *you could be threatened with consequences for not conforming.*

Take heart: Daniel was written to God's people to help them to stay faithful. So here are three lessons to learn from these three believers.

1. Self-defence is not necessary (v 16). It's good to answer questions thoughtfully, but ultimately no unbeliever stands in judgment over you—only God does. So there's no need to panic. Our responses can be calm and measured.

2. God will deliver (v 17-18). No "hand" is too strong for God to rescue us from. However dire circumstances may look, he "is able" to act.

3. Trust and persist (v 18). These men trust God to work in the way he sees fit; they may be delivered from the grave, or delivered beyond the grave. Even when God's ways seem strange to us, we must continue to say "no" to worshipping anything other than him.

❓ *Which of these three points do you find most helpful, and why?*

⌃ Pray

However many times we might fail him in the meantime, by grace and through faith we will one day be part of a crowd from every nation and language bowing down in worship to the one true God. **Read Revelation 7:9-12** and start doing that now!

❤ *Bible in a year: Isaiah 28, Isaiah 31 – 32 • Matthew 15*

Turning up the heat

It's getting hot in here. But Shadrach, Meshach and Abednego are keeping their clothes on…

Read Daniel 3:19-30

❓ *What details are we given to show that these three men are facing certain death (v 19, 20, 22, 23)?*

It looks as though Shadrach, Meshach and Abednego are beyond hope. Surely there's no way out of this one. The way the story is told sets us up to share in Nebuchadnezzar's "amazement" in verse 24.

❓ *What three surprises are there in verse 25 (compare with v 24)?*

❓ *What details are we given to show how total God's deliverance of his servants is (v 27)?*

❓ *Who does Nebuchadnezzar give the credit to (v 28-29)? What's lacking in his response, do you think?*

Who is the fourth man in the fire? Some commentators think it is a "christophany"—an Old Testament appearance of Christ—others that it is an angel. Either way, this is clearly an ambassador from heaven sent by God. As such, it reminds us that God saves by coming close; by entering into our pain; and by experiencing the judgment we are facing. All these things we see in full in the incarnation, life and death of Christ.

Shadrach, Meschach and Abednego remained faithful under trial, and God brought them out of the furnace. Jesus remained faithful under trial, and God raised him out of the tomb. And in him, we too will be brought through the fire of judgment. And so we marvel along with Nebuchadnezzar—surely "no other god can save in this way" (v 29)!

🔽 Apply

Think about some of the hard situations you're facing—perhaps ones which feel beyond hope or of which there appears to be no way out.

❓ *What difference does it make to know that…*
  • *Jesus is in the fire with you?*
  • *Christ's faithfulness means he can get you through death?*

Read 1 Peter 1:6-9. What else does God promise to be doing in the midst of your trials? How have you seen that to be true in your life previously? How does that encourage you for today?

🔼 Pray

Fear not, I am with thee; oh be not dismayed,
  For I am thy God and will still give thee aid.
I'll strengthen thee, help thee, and cause thee
    to stand,
  Upheld by My righteous, omnipotent hand.

When through fiery trials thy pathways
    shall lie,
  My grace all sufficient shall be thy supply.
The flame shall not hurt thee; I only design
  Thy dross to consume and thy gold to refine.
                (From How Firm a Foundation)

Bible in a year: Isaiah 33 – 35 • James 4 🔽

Who holds the power?

When rapper Kanye West professed faith, he released an album entitled "Jesus is King". But Daniel 4 tells the surprising conversion story of an even bigger star.

The chapter begins with a pronouncement in the voice of the king.

Axe man

Read Daniel 4:1-18

❓ *Think back over God's dealings with Nebuchadnezzar so far, as well as 4:1-8. What has the king understood about God? What has he been slow to learn?*

❓ *The king dreams of an enormous, splendid tree. Compare verses 11-12 with 14-15a. Match each element of the tree's description with what happens to it.*

❓ *In verse 18 Nebuchadnezzar asks Daniel to interpret the dream. But what hints have we already been given about:*
  • *what the dream represents (v 15b-16)?*
  • *what lesson God intends him to draw from it (v 17)?*

Ox man

Read Daniel 4:19-27

No wonder Daniel is afraid (v 19). Imagine what it would be like to deliver these words to the most powerful man in the ancient world: "Your Majesty, you are that tree!" (v 22). Soon Nebuchadnezzar will be cut down—he will lose his mind and his kingdom.

❓ *What is the big truth that the king must acknowledge (v 25, 26)?*

❓ *How should this play out in his actions (v 27)?*

To say that Nebuchadnezzar is "great and strong" (v 22) is almost an understatement. But there is a God in heaven who is greater and stronger. And God rules, not Nebuchadnezzar. Nebuchadnezzar is high, but he is not the Most High. No tree can withstand God's axe when he chooses to wield it. So Nebuchadnezzar—and everyone else—is called to acknowledge that God is King, and live in obedience to his commands (v 27).

But will Babylon's king heed Daniel's warning? We'll find that out on Monday.

☑ Apply

"The Most High is sovereign over all kingdoms on earth and gives them to anyone he wishes" (v 17, 25).

❓ *Imagine you were one of Daniel's first readers, living in Israel after their return from exile and still living in its shadow. What about that statement both encourages you and challenges you?*

❓ *Think about yourself today. What about that statement both encourages you and challenges you?*

❓ *Who would you describe as the "great and strong" trees in your world? Think personally as well as nationally/globally. What does this passage teach us about the nature of human power?*

❓ *Whether you think of yourself as a towering tree or a shaky sapling, what would it look like to live in a way that acknowledges "that Heaven rules"?*

Voice of a storm

"Quiet time." In many ways it's a helpful phrase for time with God, reading his word and praying. But it can give the idea that Bible reading is a bit tame and powerless.

And there's nothing very quiet about what happens in this psalm. Think back to the most ferocious storm you've ever encountered—David says that hearing God speak is like standing in the path of a hurricane!

This is a psalm all about encountering the Lord. David is so caught up in the wonder of God that he has put God's name in every verse except verse 6, and then twice in each of the last two verses.

Heavenly praise

Read Psalm 29:1-2

Don't get too hung up on who the "heavenly beings" are. They are powerful but created beings.

❷ *What are they called to do?*

❷ *Why are they to give glory to God? What aspects of his character are stressed here?*

A perfect storm

Read Psalm 29:3-9

The storm is pictured brewing over the Mediterranean—dark, brooding clouds, gusting winds and rumbling thunder. It moves inland over Lebanon to the north, and works its way southwards through Israel and to the desert of Kadesh beyond.

❷ *What effect does the storm have on the land as it passes through?*

❷ *How do God's people in the temple respond to this display of his might?*

❷ *What does the psalm teach us about God's words by using the storm image?*

Read Isaiah 55:10-11

Nothing can stop God's word doing God's work.

The peace of God

Read Psalm 29:10-11

After the picture of dynamic power, comes an image of settled rule. The word for "flood" appears only here and in Genesis 6 – 11. God rules over the most destructive and seemingly uncontrollable force that has ever been unleashed on this planet. How wonderful, then, to read in verse 11 that this God of flood and thunder is the God who "blesses his people with peace".

John 1:14 declares that Jesus was, and is, "the Word [who] became flesh". Jesus is not meek and mild—his is this mighty, storm-force voice of the Lord.

⌄ Apply

❷ *How does this psalm impact the way that you think about Jesus?*

❷ *How should this psalm shape the way that you think about God and his word?*

Why not pray through this psalm for the next few weeks before you go to church or read your Bible. Remind yourself of what is happening as you encounter God in his word!

Shaking the moo-ver

The US President steps off Air Force One, waving at the crowds as the press are gathered below. But as he descends the steps something strange happens…

He gets down on all fours and starts bellowing like a cow…

Nebuchadnezzar received a dream warning him to humble himself before God, or be humbled *by* God. So what will happen next? No surprises here: God said it would happen, so indeed, "all this happened…" (v 28).

Read Daniel 4:28-37

❓ *How would you describe Nebuchadnezzar's position through this passage?*
- *v 29-30*
- *v 33*
- *v 36*

❓ *What about his attitude?*
- *v 30*
- *v 34a*
- *v 34b-35, 37*

If Nebuchadnezzar were around today, we might describe him as having a "dramatic testimony". But in a sense, it is the testimony of every person who becomes a believer. It's "U" shaped: we live life singing our own praises, but in a miracle of God's grace he shows us the baseness of our sin, brings us to our senses, and causes us to look to him for rescue. Whoever we are, we must humble ourselves and ask for help in order to receive the riches of his salvation.

Indeed, the whole Christian life is "U" shaped—we live life now at the bottom of the curve, but our eyes are fixed on the glory ahead. And remarkably, we follow a Saviour who doesn't just humble people from his throne in heaven, but who humbled himself to the cross so that he might raise us up with him (Philippians 2:8-11).

This passage encourages us that if God can humble Nebuchadnezzar, and can humble us, then he can humble any of the non-Christians we know and bring them to Christ. He "does as he pleases with … the peoples of the earth" and "no one can hold back his hand" when he chooses to move in salvation (Daniel 4:35).

····· TIME OUT ·································

"No one can … say to him: 'What have you done?'" Yet so often, when we're knocked to our knees that's exactly the accusation we level at God.

Read 1 Peter 5:6

❓ *How has God used your circumstances to humble you and lift your eyes towards heaven in the past?*

❓ *How might he be seeking to do that today?*

⌃ Pray

Who do you know who seems too proud to ever come to Christ? Praise God that "those who walk in pride he is able to humble" (Daniel 4:37)—and ask him to do it!

The writing on the wall

"Like father, like son," we sometimes say. Chapter 5 introduces us to a new king of Babylon, and it's "like father, like son" in many ways… except one.

The king is Belshazzar, Nebuchadnezzar's grandson (the word translated "father" in verse 2 more generally means "ancestor" or "predecessor"). Belshazzar doesn't know it yet, but we join him on the last night of his reign, in 539 BC. That makes it around 66 years since Nebuchadnezzar had brought Daniel to Babylon.

A boozy party

Read Daniel 5:1-4

❷ *Flick back and compare…*
  • *5:1-4 with 1:2. Why are Belshazzar's actions incredibly offensive?*
  • *5:4 with 2:31-35. Why are Belshazzar's actions incredibly foolish?*

Picture the scene of raucous excess as Belshazzar and his guests mockingly raise Yahweh's goblets to false "gods". *Ha! Who is this Jewish non-god and where is he now?* But while Belshazzar is getting smashed, he does not realise he is actually about to *be* smashed…

Suddenly sober…

Read Daniel 5:5-17

❷ *What similarities do we see between this passage and chapter 4? Compare:*
  • *5:5-6 and 4:4-5*
  • *5:7 and 4:6-7*
  • *5:10-16 and 4:8-9*

❷ *How does Belshazzar show his arrogance in 5:13-16?*

The king offers Daniel honour and riches, but God's messenger is not to be bought (v 17). The writer is inviting us to draw a direct comparison between chapter 4 and 5. Both kings receive a revelation from God that makes them afraid and is beyond the understanding of their advisors. Both kings call on Daniel for an interpretation. But as we'll see tomorrow, the outcome for each king could not be more different: one king God humbles in salvation, the other king he humbles with judgment. Throughout the Bible, the two come together. Here in Daniel 5, Belshazzar's death will pave the way for a new king who will release God's people from exile and allow them home (Ezra 1:1-3). Salvation and judgment are two sides of the same coin—and God is sovereign in both.

⌄ Apply

❷ *Who are the "gods" that the non-believers you know "raise a toast" to?*

❷ *When we remember that it is the Lord who rules, how does this show their behaviour to be arrogant, foolish and offensive to God?*

❷ *What difference would it make to you today if you truly believed that their "party" could end tonight?*

Pray again for the non-Christian you prayed for yesterday, asking God to graciously show them the error of their ways before it's too late.

Numbered and weighed

Belshazzar's feast is about to come to an abrupt ending. The writing's on the wall for the king and his friends. Literally...

The charge

Read Daniel 5:18-24

- ❓ *How do Daniel's words underline for us (again) the point of chapter 4?*
- ❓ *Belshazzar "knew all this" (5:22). What should he have done? What did he do instead?*

The sentence

Read Daniel 5:25-31

- ❓ *What is God's judgment on Belshazzar?*
- ❓ *How does Belshazzar take the news (v 29)?*
- ❓ *What's striking about verses 30-31? How is this different from the way that chapter 4 ended?*

Nebuchadnezzar's humiliation led to his restoration—when we said goodbye to him at the end of chapter 4, he resolved to "praise and exalt and glorify the King of heaven". Belshazzar's humiliation ends only in judgment. Why? Because he refused to repent. He knew about God's dealings with his grandfather (Daniel 5:22), and yet refused to honour God himself (v 23). Even in verse 29, he's still acting as if he's got power to give away! So God moves quickly in judgment—"that very night" Belshazzar lost not just his kingdom, but his life (v 30-31).

···· TIME OUT ··

Read Romans 1:18-25

- ❓ *What similarities do you see between Belshazzar's behaviour in Daniel 5, and what Paul says is true of all humanity in Romans 1?*

⌄ Apply

There's a warning here to all of us who have heard the gospel. *Hearing is not enough.* We may know "all this"—but have we responded in genuine, humble repentance? Have we bowed the knee before God, or set ourselves up against him? Do we acknowledge that it is God who holds "in his hand your life and all your ways" (Daniel 5:23), or do we continue to act as though we call the shots?

It's right to fear for people we love who have heard and ignored God's warning. "It is a dreadful thing to fall into the hands of the living God" (Hebrews 10:31). So we pray all the more fervently, and speak of Jesus all the more earnestly.

These truths are hard to read. Yet at the same time, we acknowledge that God "does as he pleases with the powers of heaven and the peoples of the earth" (Daniel 4:35). He has the right to save, and he has the right to judge. "No one can hold back his hand or say to him: 'What have you done?'" (v 35). Instead we stand in fear, awe and amazement that he would save us. And it humbles us further still. We too were "without excuse"—yet "while we were still sinners, Christ died for us" (Romans 1:20; 5:8).

Praying by the window

Daniel is now an old man in his 80s. But far from winding down for an easy retirement, he's about to face his toughest test yet.

Read Daniel 6:1-12

❓ *Why and how do the administrators and satraps conspire against Daniel?*

❓ *How would you describe Daniel's response? What does that tell us about his character, and his habits?*

⌄ Apply

Daniel was written as an example of faithfulness for God's people—then as now.

❓ *"We will never find any basis for charges against this man/woman _____ unless it has something to do with..." If that sentence were being said of you, how would it end?*

❓ *What would it look like to use your gifts with such excellence and integrity that the only charge against you could be "something to do with" your God"?*

Daniel's courage is remarkable. When he hears about the "prayer ban", he goes home, opens wide his window... and prays anyway. (Three times a day—more than many of us do with no such ban in place!)

There will, perhaps, be just a few key moments in our lives when we're faced with an overt and costly choice between conformity with the world and obedience to God like this. So how can we become the kind of people who would go home, open wide the window, and pray, even when commanded not to?

Answer: by being the kind of people who go home, open wide the window, and pray on every other day before that. Daniel was doing "just as he had done before" (v 10). Decades of daily faithfulness had prepared him for this test.

❓ *How does that encourage and challenge you as you endeavour to read the Bible and pray day-by-day, and as you choose obedience over conformity in the little things?*

Read Daniel 6:13-18

❓ *What similarities do you see between Daniel 6 and the way that Jesus was tried and condemned to death? (See Matthew 26:59-60; 27:11-26, 57-66.)*

If this passage has left you conscious of your failures, let it also make you conscious of your Saviour. Jesus lived a life of such perfect obedience that no charge could be made to stick; he silently submitted himself to the decree of a weak and conflicted human ruler; he was sealed in a stone tomb. He was faithful unto death so that he could rescue a faithless people from death. In the words of an old Easter hymn, "Hallelujah! What a Saviour!"

And Daniel? As in any Old Testament passage, the human isn't the hero—God is. So will Daniel's God be able to rescue him from death? Like King Darius, we'll have to wait until tomorrow to find out...

The mane thing

Darius has spent a sleepless night in the palace, while Daniel has spent a night in the lions' den. Try to imagine you don't know what happens next...

❓ *Look back at verses 12-18. What details are we given to make sure we know that Daniel's situation is really, really bad?*

Read Daniel 6:19-24

❓ *What's the (surprise!) answer to Darius' question of verse 20?*

❓ *Why did God rescue Daniel (v 22-23)?*

❓ *What does the gruesome detail of verse 24 add to our understanding, do you think?*

Verse 24 makes for difficult reading (and is mostly left out of the kids' picture books...). At the very least, it shows us that Daniel's rescue was no accident! And more importantly, it reminds us that God deals in great reversals: at the end of the day, God's man will be vindicated, and God's enemies destroyed. The one who looked doomed to destruction is rescued, and the ones who think they're on top are judged.

It's the same with the gospel story: Jesus was raised from the grave—"lifted from the den"—because he was innocent in God's sight (Acts 5:29-32). He didn't falsely claim to be God's King—he really was God's King, and the resurrection proved it. He submitted himself to death and was brought through to life because, like Daniel, he "trusted in his God" (Daniel 6:23).

Verse 24 is a sobering picture of the fate that all humanity—all God's enemies—deserve. But... *God rescues.* When we trust in

Christ we are included "in Christ"—his innocence becomes our innocence, his vindication becomes our vindication, and his resurrection secures our resurrection. Until that day, we too may face earthly enemies who conspire to do us ill. We certainly face a spiritual enemy, the devil, who seeks to devour us like a roaring lion (1 Peter 5:8). But like Daniel, we continue in obedience and with confidence in the God who reverses fortunes and rescues his people.

Read Daniel 6:25-28

❓ *What other great reversal do we see here (compare with v 7-9)?*

❓ *What's the moral of the story according to Darius?*

❓ *Do you think he's got it right?*

❓ *What's the appropriate response to a God who rescues (start of v 26)?*

❓ *What would that look like for you?*

🔼 Pray

Turn Darius' decree in verses 26-27 into your own song of praise to the living God who rescues and saves people.

Weird but wonderful

We're about to enter into what you might think of as "the weird half" of the book of Daniel. It may be weird—but it's definitely wonderful.

Besides, while the book does neatly divide into two halves of narrative (chapters 1 – 6) and prophecy (chapters 7 –12), today's reading still belongs to the section written in Aramaic (2:4 – 7:28).

Read Daniel 7:1-8

❓ *When does Daniel receive this vision (v 1)? What do we know about life under this king (including for Daniel) from chapter 5?*

❓ *What are the first three beasts "like" (7:4, 5, 6)? What is different (and more terrifying) about the fourth (v 7-8)?*

Daniel is told in verse 17 that these four beasts represent four kingdoms "that will rise from the earth". They probably represent the same four kingdoms as the sections of the statue from chapter 2. Daniel's dream mirrors Nebuchadnezzar's in several interesting ways, with each serving as bookends to the book's Aramaic section (flick back and compare them if you have time).

But more generally, the four beasts can be taken to represent all human powers; notice the distorted human features of each.

❓ *What does Daniel 7:1-8 show us about the nature of fallen human power (e.g. where does it come from and what does it do; what feelings do these visions evoke)?*

❓ *Where and how have you seen "beastly" human powers in the world around you?*

The scene is chaotic, destructive and utterly terrifying. But then in verse 9 the camera angle pans to show us the divine power that stands above all human powers...

Read Daniel 7:9-14

The "son of man" in verses 13-14 is, of course, the Lord Jesus—we'll think in more detail about this part of the vision tomorrow.

❓ *What contrasts do you see between the beasts and the Ancient of Days (e.g. where they come from, how long they last, what happens to them, their interaction with people)?*

❓ *Think back over the book of Daniel: where else have we seen this difference between human authority and God's authority?*

However it might appear to the contrary, the Ancient of Days is on the throne!

❓ *Why is it good news that this God rules?*

❓ *What would be an appropriate response (e.g. v 10, 14)?*

⌃ Pray

Talk to God about your answer to those final questions. Depending on your age and Christian experience, you might also enjoy responding to today's passage by listening to the 90s worship song "Ancient of Days" by Ron Kenoly.

Bible in a year: Isaiah 58 – 60 • Revelation 21 ⌄

From pride to praise

Do you find that you pray to and rely on God more when life is going well, or when you are facing difficulties and challenges?

There are spiritual dangers in both experiences, but perhaps it is when life is comfortable that we are most likely to forget God, as we feel no pressing need for him.

What I learned

Read Psalm 30:1-5

We don't know what particular experience David is writing about here. He spent much of his early life on the run from people who wanted to kill him.

> ❷ *What images does he use to describe God's rescue here?*

Note that when the king is rescued, all the people praise God (v 4). Of course, this is even more true for us as we trust in great David's greater son, Jesus. His resurrection rescue means eternal life and eternal rejoicing for his people (1 Corinthians 15:20-28).

How I learned it

Read Psalm 30:6-12

It's easy to miss what's wrong in verse 6!

> ❷ *But where is David's confidence when life is secure and good? (Hint: Who is not mentioned in verse 6?)*
> ❷ *What then happens when God strips away his security and allows him to face danger in verses 7-10?*
> ❷ *What does God's rescue in verse 11 lead him to do in verse 12?*

The heart of this psalm is the series of contrasting pairs that fill verses 5 and 11.

> ❷ *What are those contrasts?*

For some of us, we will be able to look back on times in our walk with Christ when we have had experiences like this—perhaps our conversion or a time when God rescued us from a terrible situation. For others of us, perhaps it feels as if we are still in verses 7-8.

Remember, too, that, as Christians we have experienced a far greater rescue than David talks of here. Our enemy was the devil. Our certain destiny was death. But God rescued us through the death and resurrection of Jesus Christ. So even if we haven't known an experience that fulfils this psalm "to the letter", we have known a rescue that fulfils it "to the better".

⌃ Pray

Pray through the contrasts of verses 5 and 11, knowing that ultimately, eternally, this will be true for all who trust in Jesus. Pray for trust in Jesus while you live through the weeping of the night.

Pray too for others you know who are in the middle of the battle with suffering, and need strength to trust God as they wait for the day of joy and dancing.

Think about your salvation, and use the phrases of this psalm to thank God for that rescue from sin and death.

The son of man...

The phrase "Son of Man" is used over 80 times in the Gospels, mostly by Jesus as a title for himself. Today we'll look at just two examples.

Read Daniel 7:13-14

❷ *Where is the son of man going? What does he receive, and from whom?*

❷ *How does this compare to the figures in verses 2-7, 11-12?*

This vision describes Christ's "coronation" in heaven, following his ascension, when he returned to his Father (see Acts 1:1-11). Philippians 2:6-11 tells us that having humbled himself to death, "God exalted him to the highest place and gave him the name that is above every name, that at the name of Jesus every knee should bow" (v 9-10).

... who serves...

Read Mark 10:42-45

❷ *Given what the disciples would have known about "the Son of Man" from Daniel 7, what would have been surprising about Jesus' words here?*

Daniel 7 shows us the Son of Man in all his glory—but the New Testament reveals that suffering always comes before exaltation. Of course, as one person of the Trinity, God the Son has always been totally worthy of glory and honour and worship. But there is something in his servanthood—his ransom-paying, sin-defeating, freedom-bringing death on the cross—which leads to a glory that is greater than before (see again Philippians 2:6-11). Far from diminishing his greatness and glory, his humble service makes us love and worship him all the more.

✅ Apply

❷ *If "even" the Son of Man came not to be served but to serve, how should that affect how we conduct ourselves?*

❷ *In what ways are you tempted to "lord it over" other people? (Think about your speech, actions and attitudes—at home, at church, at work, and with your friends.)*

❷ *What would it look like to be a "slave of all" today instead?*

... and judges

Read Mark 14:60-64

❷ *What is shocking about Jesus' claim in verse 62 given what the high priest would have known from Daniel 7?*

Whereas Daniel 7 describes the Son of Man coming into his Father's presence, here Jesus uses similar language to describe his second "coming" to earth. The two are closely linked: Jesus is King and Judge because he has been given "authority, glory and sovereign power" over "all nations and peoples of every language".

🔼 Pray

Daniel 7 describes an as-yet unseen reality—but one day every knee will bow before him, and every tongue acknowledge that Jesus Christ is Lord (Philippians 2:10-11).

Bible in a year: Isaiah 61 – 62 • Ezekiel 36 • Romans 2 ⬇

Wondering about signs

So far it's been troubled kings who have come to Daniel for interpretations. But now it's Daniel who needs to seek out an interpreter for his troubling dreams.

Daniel has seen a vision in which several different images passed through his mind: four strange beasts, the last of which is "terrifying and frightening and very powerful" (7:7); God's holy throneroom; the destruction of the fourth beast; and the exaltation of one who looks like "a son of man" (7:13). *But what does it all mean?*

The meaning

Read Daniel 7:15-18

❷ *Look at verse 18. What's surprising about who possesses the kingdom for ever?*

❷ *What might you expect it to say, given verses 13-14?*

Here's the extraordinary truth: in eternity we won't just be worshipping the Son of Man—we will be reigning *with* the Son of Man: "If we died with him, we will also live with him; if we endure, we will also reign with him" (2 Timothy 2:11-12). As the perfect man and second Adam, Christ restores his people to do the job humanity failed at first time round, as we rule over a new creation (see Genesis 1:26-31).

The scene at the end of C.S. Lewis's *The Lion, the Witch and Wardrobe*, where Aslan crowns the children Kings and Queens of Narnia, gives us a sense of the honour and privilege ahead of us.

But before that day, life is not going to be easy for God's people...

The hope

Read Daniel 7:19-28

❷ *What will life be like for God's holy people under the rule of these kings (v 19, 21, 25)?*

❷ *What hope is there (v 22, 26-27)?*

❷ *Remember when and where Daniel receives this vision (7:1). What message does God have for him (and his readers after him), do you think?*

Four kingdoms, ten kings, and one final king who will be worst of all... It's tempting to try to map these figures onto individual empires and kings throughout history. (The final king seems to correspond to the ultimate Antichrist/Man of Lawlessness of the end of history, see 2 Thessalonians 2:1-10.) But it's more helpful to see in this vision a general pattern for God's people living before the return of Christ: human powers will oppress us, but only for "a time" (Daniel 7:25). The date is set for their destruction. Evil will not win. The Most High rules, and one day his people will reign.

⌃ Pray

There's a promise of a happy ending, but Daniel is still left "deeply troubled" (v 28). We cannot be glib about the suffering of God's people. Instead, spend time in serious prayer for persecuted Christians around the world today.

Bible in a year: Isaiah 64 – 66 • 1 Corinthians 2

The grand design

Daniel's vision in chapter 7 (written in Aramaic) concerned the big sweep of history, from the Babylonian Empire to the second coming of Christ.

The vision in chapter 8 (written in Hebrew) reveals what will happen in a specific period of Israel's history.

Read Daniel 8:1-4

Note the time and place (v 1-2). Susa was the capital of Persia, and the ram, we're told in verse 20, represents the Medo-Persian Empire (the one that will come after Belshazzar's Babylon).

❓ *What is impressive about the ram?*

Read Daniel 8:5-8

❓ *What happens next to the ram? Retell it in your own words—try to be as vivid as Daniel is here!*

Verses 21-22 tell us that the goat represents Greece. The first horn represents Alexander the Great. During his short but wildly successful reign, he overthrew the Persian Empire and expanded his territory all the way from Egypt in the west to India in the east (v 5-7). But in 323 BC Alexander died suddenly in Babylon, and a power struggle between four of his generals followed (v 8).

From the line of one of these generals would rise a particular king who would bring trouble on God's people...

Read Daniel 8:9-14

❓ *What is particularly appalling about this king?*

Remember, the first readers of the book of Daniel had returned home to Israel ("the

Beautiful Land", v 9), after 70 years in exile. They had worked hard to rebuild their nation, and their temple. How distressing then to hear that history will repeat itself as a foreign power desecrates the temple and tramples God's people, just as the Babylonians had in Daniel 1. But we'll see tomorrow that they are given a glimmer of hope.

⌄ Apply

Looking back from our point in history, we can see how each of the details of this vision came true. This leaves us with a very simple, but very important, point of application: *what God says will happen, will happen.* Why? Because he is in control of history, from the grand narrative to the small details of "evenings and mornings" (8:14).

❓ *What things that God has said will happen in his word are you tempted to doubt? How does what you have read in Daniel 8 speak to that?*

Daniel's vision focuses on the years 334 – 164 BC, but God extends the same level of detailed control over every period of human history, including all the decades of your lifetime.

❓ *As you think about your slice of human history, are you dismayed or encouraged? What difference does it make to know that God rules over every day of it?*

Troubling times

Does watching the news ever make you feel weary? In his visions, Daniel is watching something so appalling that he's left flat on his back, exhausted…

The final horn

Read Daniel 8:15-26

❓ *Look at verses 23-25. What further details are we given about the final horn of verses 9-12? What will he be like?*

❓ *What is the one glimmer of hope in this otherwise grim future for God's people (see v 25)?*

❓ *Where will rescue come from?*

The king in question is the Greek Antiochus IV Epiphanes (175 – 164 BC). The title Epiphanes means "God Manifest", but some people at the time gave him the nickname Epimanes "The Mad One". That tells you plenty about this man's attitude and actions!

Antiochus reversed a more tolerant policy towards the province of Judea, and used his power to forbid the worship of the Lord, install those of his choice as high priest, raid the temple treasury to finance his campaigns, and even build a pagan altar in the temple. The persecution eventually led to a revolt led by Judas Maccabeus, which is celebrated each year in the Jewish festival of Hanukkah. This gives us an idea of what the Jews of his day were expecting of Jesus, a couple of centuries later. Antiochus died suddenly in 164 BC. Both history and Scripture (Daniel 7:27) point to the same truth: *God rules.*

Exhausted by evil

Read Daniel 8:27

❓ *How does Daniel respond to this vision (see also v 15, 18)?*

⌄ Apply

If, like Daniel, you are trying (and perhaps failing!) to understand what's going on in chapter 8, here's the big picture: God's people *will* face persecution. We see it in history, we see it globally today, and perhaps we even experience it personally.

If you feel worn out and exhausted by the evil in the world that rages against God and his people, even when it does not directly affect you, then you're in good company— Daniel did too. Life in this world, until Jesus returns, really can be horrifying, and it's right to feel the force of that. But God meets us in our distress, and with his strengthening touch he helps us to stand by his Spirit through his word. **Read 1 Peter 5:10-11.**

But then, like Daniel, we need to get up and get on with "the king's business" (Daniel 7:27) until the true King comes again.

⌃ Pray

Cry out to God about the victims of evil who are on your heart; pray for his strength to stand firm; and ask him to help you to do what needs doing today.

"We deserved it"

It's 539 BC, and there's a new king on the throne: Darius the Mede. So chronologically, chapter 9 comes shortly after the overthrow of Belshazzar in 5:30-31.

The sins of our fathers
Read Daniel 9:1-3; Jeremiah 25:8-12

❓ *What does Daniel realise is significant about this time?*

❓ *What is interesting about his response?*

After (roughly) 70 years in exile, it looks like God's word in Jeremiah 25:12 is beginning to be fulfilled: Babylon has fallen. So is it time for Daniel to pack his bags and throw a farewell party? *Nope...* Instead of putting the prosecco on ice, Daniel dons sackcloth, fasts, and mourns the sin that led to the exile in the first place.

Read Daniel 9:4-14

❓ *Pick out everything we're told about...*
  • God's deeds and character.
  • his people's deeds and character.

In Deuteronomy 28, as the people prepared to enter the promised land, God set out the terms of his covenant agreement with them. It was pretty simple: if they obeyed him, he would bless them; if they disobeyed him, they would experience his curse. The rest of the Old Testament is essentially the story of God's total faithfulness to his end of the deal, and the people's total failure to keep theirs. After ignoring God's warnings for centuries, they were indeed "uprooted from the land" and "[scattered] among all nations" (Deuteronomy 28:63-64). So Daniel holds up his hands and says, *It's a fair cop. We deserve to be here* (Daniel 9:14).

❓ *Why was this relevant to Daniel's first readers, living back in the land after the exile, do you think?*

⌄ Apply

This is our God: faithful, righteous, merciful. This is us by nature: wicked, rebellious, unfaithful, refusing to listen or obey.

But not anymore. We don't live in Deuteronomy 28; we live in Hebrews 8. Christ is the mediator of a new covenant which is "superior to the old one, since the new covenant is established on better promises" (v 6); a promise of new minds and new hearts (v 10), brought about by the blood of our high priest, Jesus (v 1; see also Luke 22:20).

❓ *Given Daniel 9:4-14, why is this very good news for us?*

❓ *Do you, like Daniel, accept that you deserve God's judgment? Or do you jump to celebrate God's rescue in a way that suggests you think you deserve it really?*

⌃ Pray

Daniel trusts that God will do as he has said; but there is not a hint of presumption. These two attitudes find their balance in the way that he prays according to God's word, humbly asking God to do what he has promised. Do that now, with confession and petition.

Why bother praying?

"If God already knows what he's going to do, why bother praying?" Most of us have asked, or been asked, that question at some stage.

The Israelites have been in exile for 70 years. Yesterday we listened as Daniel confessed that he and his people deserved every single day of it. But there's room for hope yet...

Read Daniel 9:15-19

❓ *Daniel is asking God to bring an end to the exile and restore his people to their land. To what does he appeal in...*
- *v 16?*
- *v 17?*
- *v 18?*
- *v 19?*

First, Daniel appeals to *God's mercy* (v 16, 18). God kept his word by moving against Israel in judgment; now Daniel appeals to God to keep his word by turning away his anger. God promises to judge those who disobey him; but he promises to show mercy to those who repent. He is faithful to his people ("your city, your holy hill") even when they are faithless. *Why?* Because he is righteous, so he keeps his word. 1 John 1:9 says something similar: "If we confess our sins, he is faithful and just and will forgive us our sins".

Second, Daniel appeals to *God's glory* (Daniel 9:17, 19). At the exodus, God "made ... a name" for himself by parting the Red Sea and rescuing his people; all the nations around saw that Israel's God was the most powerful (v 15). But now the Lord's city lies in ruins, his temple abandoned, and his people in exile. He looks distinctly less

powerful. So Daniel asks God to act again, so that everyone will see how great he is.

The New Testament is likewise full of prayers for God to be glorified. Paul prays that the Christians in Philippi would love more and live blamelessly "to the glory and praise of God" (Philippians 1:9-11). Whether it's salvation or sanctification, none of it is really about us: it's all about God.

···· TIME OUT ·······································

So did God answer Daniel? Tomorrow, we'll read about a vision that God gave to Daniel in reply. But today, **read Ezra 1:1-4** to see God work in history to answer Daniel's prayer too. (Note that Darius and Cyrus are possibly two names for the same person.)

⌄ Apply

❓ *Think about how your prayers normally sound. Do they appeal to God's mercy, God's glory, or something else?*

❓ *"If God already knows what he's going to do, why bother praying?" Having read Daniel's prayer in Daniel 9:4-19, how would you answer that question now?*

⌃ Pray

Pray for some of the personal qualities and people that you regularly pray for, but in a way which specifically appeals to God's mercy and glory.

Expressing emotions

Why do people drink heavily when tragedy strikes? In part it is to dull the pain. But I wonder if it is also because we don't know how to express our feelings while sober.

Being drunk enables us to blurt out what we don't know how to say. Still, drunken blurting out is not a sign of emotional health—yet neither is soberly bottling it all up. One of the blessings of the psalms is that they enable us to express and process our emotions in a healthy way. And that is true of this perplexing psalm of David.

Hunted but trusting

Read Psalm 31:1-8

❓ *How does David describe his situation?*

❓ *What truths about God does he rely on?*

❓ *What specific things does he ask for?*

Abandoned but comforted

It seems as if all is resolved (v 7-8), but then we're back to danger and despair (v 9-13).

Read Psalm 31:9-13

I read this psalm on the morning after the Paris terror attacks in November 2015. I was grateful that these ancient prayers are so relevant to life today, as I could not find my own words to pray in the light of all the tragedy and uncertainty of that horror, and the news that terror really was "on every side".

Read Psalm 31:14-18

Verses 14-15 are the hinge in this psalm.

❓ *What truths in particular does David preach to himself here?*

❓ *How are they encouraging to you today?*

Confident and praising

Read Psalm 31:19-24

David ends by celebrating God's goodness (v 19-20) and his experience of it (v 21-22).

❓ *This leads him to call on God's people to do what (v 23-24)?*

Part of the purpose of the history of God's dealings with his people—and part of the joy of reflecting on God's dealing with us individually—is to encourage us to "be strong and take heart" and "hope in the LORD!" But there's more for us here—because as Jesus died on the cross, he prayed verse 5 (Luke 23:46). Think about the rest of Psalm 31—in particular how it ends in verses 19-24.

❓ *How does this help shape your understanding of what Jesus meant as he prayed that briefest of prayers?*

Jesus prayed this psalm and endured such darkness for us. No matter how confusing and dangerous our lives are, Jesus our Saviour is there with us. Better still, we find he has been there before us and emerged to resurrection life on the other side.

⌃ Pray

Acknowledge to God that "my times are in your hands" (v 15). Commit your life and all those you love into his hands (v 5). Pray that you and they would "be strong and take heart" and "hope in the LORD" (v 24).

The unfolding plan

Do you ever pray and feel as if God's not listening? Today's verses encourage us that he is.

Heard

Read Daniel 9:20-23

> ❷ *What's the time gap between Daniel praying, and God...*
> • *hearing?*
> • *answering?*

The first is guaranteed: when we pray, God always hears us. The answer may not be immediate (in 10:2 Daniel prays for three weeks; in Nehemiah 1:4, Nehemiah prays for "some days"), but we have *always* been heard. And regardless of whether and when God gives us the thing we ask for, we can be encouraged that God gives "insight and understanding" to prayerful people (Daniel 9:22; see James 1:5).

⌃ Pray

With that in mind, spend some time talking to God now—perhaps about some of those requests that it feels like he isn't listening to. Rejoice that he hears; ask him to act in his timing; and pray that God would fill you with wisdom and understanding as you persevere in prayer.

Answered

Read Daniel 9:24

This is the "summary answer" to Daniel's prayer. Gabriel lifts Daniel's eyes beyond the end of exile to an even greater rescue...

> ❷ *In what sense did/will Christ achieve each of the things listed in this verse?*

"Seven" is probably symbolic of completeness, rather than a specific number of weeks or years. The following verses give more details on how the "seventy 'sevens'" will play out.

Read Daniel 9:25-27

> ❷ *The 70 sevens are broken down into three time periods. What will happen...*
> • *during the 7 "sevens" (end of v 25)?*
> • *after the 62 "sevens" (start of v 26)?*
> • *during the final "seven" (v 27)?*

One interpretation is that these represent: the rebuilding of the Jerusalem temple and walls under Ezra and Nehemiah; the 400 years of "prophetic silence" that followed the completion of the city before the arrival of the "Anointed One", Jesus; and the time from Jesus' death and resurrection to his return, during which worship in the temple would cease (when it was destroyed by Titus in AD 70), and life will be hard for his people.

Verse 27 reads as though the "Anointed One" will set up the abomination—but we know that can't be Jesus! The end of verse 27 could instead correspond to the "people" at the end of verse 26 (the ruler's own people who turn against him). But the images and ideas seem a little jumbled here.

Even if there are things here we don't understand, there is still plenty to encourage us—so praise God for those things now.

Dark forces at work

Behind our internet browser lies a hidden world of big tech companies, powerful forces and mysterious algorithms that few of us know much about.

Occasionally, a scandal breaks which shows us that there's far more going on than we realise—some of it malign. The final vision given to Daniel, which stretches across chapters 10 – 12, takes us behind the scenes of this world to give us a glimpse of the powerful spiritual forces at work.

Be afraid...

Read Daniel 10:1-9

❓ *When does Daniel receive this vision, and why is that significant (v 1, 2-3)?*

The first exiles were sent home in the first year of Cyrus (see Ezra 1:1-3), but it's not exactly been plain sailing since. So back in Babylon, Daniel devotes himself to fasting and prayer. He wants to understand what lies ahead for God's people. And God answers...

❓ *What is impressive about the man Daniel sees (Daniel 10:5-6)?*

❓ *Look at verses 7-9. On a scale of 1-10, how frightened is Daniel?!*

Who is this "man"? The similarities with the "son of man" John sees in Revelation 1:12-18, and the "son of man" in Daniel 7, mean that we can be pretty sure that this is a pre-incarnate appearance of Jesus.

Don't be afraid...

Read Daniel 10:10-14

❓ *What does the Lord say/do to help Daniel to not be afraid (v 10, 11, 12)?*

❓ *Why has he come to Daniel (v 12, 14)?*

❓ *Daniel started praying three weeks before. What has the Lord been doing since then (v 13)?*

We've seen human powers come and go in the book of Daniel, and some who have oppressed God's people. Yet behind the scenes of this world a spiritual battle is taking place between the forces of evil—captained by "the prince of this world", the devil (John 14:30), and the forces of light—captained by our mighty champion, King Jesus. This glimpse of unseen realities ought to, like Daniel, drive us to our knees in prayer.

Yet while the battle is fierce, the end is not in doubt: God knows what will happen "in the future" (Daniel 10:14). Colossians 2:15 assures us that Christ has "disarmed the powers and authorities ... [and] made a public spectacle of them, triumphing over them by the cross".

◤ Pray

"Since the first day that you set your mind to gain understanding and to humble yourself before your God, your words were heard."
                                    (Daniel 10:12)

Let this verse inspire you to pray humbly, earnestly and confidently.

Bible in a year: Jeremiah 11 – 14 ⬥

The prince of Persia

Daniel has been startled by a terrifying vision of a shining, fiery man… and then comforted with a touch and told not to be afraid.

The Lord has come "to explain to you [Daniel] what will happen to your people in the future" (v 14). It's a vision that will take us through to the end of the book. But is Daniel ready for it?

Be strong

Read Daniel 10:15 – 11:1

❓ *How would you say Daniel is feeling at this moment (10:15-17)?*

❓ *What is it that helps (v 16, 18-19)?*

Having reiterated his comfort to Daniel, the Lord then repeats why and under what circumstances he has come (10:20 – 11:1): he is in the middle of a spiritual battle, but has come to tell Daniel what will happen. It's a future that is certain, because it has been determined by God and written in his "book".

···· TIME OUT ···

The New Testament helps to fill out our understanding of spiritual warfare.

Read Ephesians 6:10-20

❓ *What does this passage tell us about…*
  • *who/what we're fighting against (v 11-12)?*
  • *how to stand firm (v 10-11, 13-17)?*
  • *the role of prayer in spiritual warfare (v 18-20)?*

❓ *What similarities do you see between this passage and what we've read in Daniel 10?*

Apply

Perhaps, like Daniel, the reality of your sin and circumstances is crushing. And perhaps the thought of meeting God face to face leaves you feeling weak, anguished, speechless; your face in the dust. That's ok. The vision that Daniel is about to see reminds us that life as one of God's people is not easy. That was true for Daniel, true for his first readers, and true for us today. Weakness is allowed.

But in our weakness, our Lord Jesus meets us with his strength. He is infinitely strong, but infinitely gentle. We are "highly esteemed"—loved by him and precious to him. Through his Spirit, we can experience his touch; hear his voice through his word; feel his peace and strength in our hearts. He alone is the place to go for the spiritual resources we need.

When we can't bear to hear, he will help us to listen; when we can't find the words, he will help us to speak; when it feels as though we'll be washed away, he will make sure we stand firm.

Pray

"Peace! Be strong now; be strong."

In what circumstances do you particularly need to hear this? Ask the Lord Jesus to give you strength.

Future sight

In answer to Daniel's prayer, the Lord is about to give him a detailed rundown of the news headlines for the next few hundred years of history.

Setting the stage

Read Daniel 11:2-4

These verses concern the same period of history as Daniel 8:1-8, 19-22. Try to match up which bits of the vision in Daniel 8 correspond to which details in Daniel 11:2-4.

The "mighty king" from Greece (11:3) is Alexander the Great, who ruled 336-323 BC. After him, his kingdom was divided between four warring generals (v 4), of whom Ptolemy and Seleucus became dominant. They and their descendants are described in Daniel 11 as "the king of the South" (in Egypt) and "the king of the North" (in Syria) respectively.

Let battle commence

Read Daniel 11:7-20

❷ *As you read, mark with arrows below who is attacking who:*

King of the North

King of the South

❷ *How would you describe these two dynasties? (What repeated attitudes, themes and ideas do you see?)*

❷ *To what extent would you say that this is also true of the powers dominating our news headlines today?*

Look at a map, and you'll see that Israel is wedged right between these two kingdoms—so every battle between these two kings means troops on Israel's turf.

❷ *What do you think it would have been like to have been an Israelite living through this period of history? What difference would having Daniel's prophecy have made?*

These verses describe a relatively brief period of history in remarkable detail. For example, verse 6 predicts the marriage of Ptolemy II's daughter Berenice to the Seleucid king Antiochus II in around 250 BC. Verse 17 describes how Antiochus III's daughter Cleopatra would marry Ptolemy V —and then switch loyalties from her father to her husband. Northern King Antiochus III then went on to attack the coastal towns and Greek islands in Asia Minor, only to be defeated by a Roman "commander", Lucius Cornelius Scipio, in 190 BC (v 18).

Read it as history, and it's interesting. But read it as prophecy, and it's miraculous. What an incredible book the Bible is! And that's because it's written for us by an incredible God—one who governs history in every detail, right down to every political marriage.

❷ *When you next read, watch or listen to the news, what will you remind yourself of from Daniel 11?*

Bible in a year: Jeremiah 21 – 22, Jeremiah 24 • John 14 ⌄

Who wins?

Yesterday's headline: God's people will be caught in the middle of a terrible north/south battle (v 2-20). Today's headline: Then things will get even worse...

Contemptible ruler

Read Daniel 11:21-28

❓ *What kind of words would you use to describe this king?*

❓ *Why is he particularly bad news for God's people (v 22, 28)?*

As in the vision in Daniel 8, the ruler in view here is Antiochus IV. Flick back to Explore Day 74 to remind yourself of who he was and what he did.

❓ *What hope is there for Daniel's first readers during his rule (11:24, 27)?*

❓ *How does this fit with the big themes we keep seeing in Daniel?*

Covenant people

Read Daniel 11:29-35

❓ *How will Antiochus "turn up the heat" on God's people?*

After a failed attack on Egypt in 168 BC (v 29-30), Antiochus intensified his persecution of the people of Jerusalem, leading to the desecration of the temple in 167 BC. While the armed resistance of Judas Maccabeus provided "a little help" (v 34), it was God's intervention "at the appointed time" (v 27) that would ultimately bring relief.

❓ *In what different ways will people respond to the pressure (v 32-35)?*

Notice how God's faithful people are described: as those "who know their God" (v 32) and as "those who are wise" (v 33). If you want to be someone who stands firm under pressure, it will come from knowing God, trusting his character, and walking with him day by day. Worldly wisdom will tell us to throw in our lot with whoever looks to be on top—but true wisdom stays faithful to God, even when it costs (v 33).

The gates of hell may rage against God's people; but Christ has said he will build his church (Matthew 16:18). And as Daniel has shown us, God's words always come true. Regardless of whatever anyone may do to us in the meantime, if we cling to Christ we are sure to one day stand before him refined, pure and spotless (Daniel 11:35); white-robed worshippers around God's throne "who have come out of the great tribulation; they have washed their robes and made them white in the blood of the Lamb" (Revelation 7:14).

⌃ Pray

And though this world, with devils filled,
 Should threaten to undo us,
We will not fear, for God hath willed
 His truth to triumph through us.
The Prince of Darkness grim,
 We tremble not for him;
His rage we can endure,
 For lo! his doom is sure,
 One little word shall fell him.

A Mighty Fortress is Our God,
Martin Luther

Caught in the crossfire

In Daniel's vision, the man dressed in linen continues to describe the exploits of a "contemptible" ruler in the north.

The heart of sin

Read Daniel 11:36-39

❓ *What attitude is at the heart of this man's sinful actions (v 36, 37)?*

❓ *In what sense is this the attitude behind all sin, do you think? Where do you see it...*
- *elsewhere in the Bible?*
- *around you today?*
- *in yourself?*

When the snake tempted Eve to eat the forbidden fruit in the Garden of Eden, he did so with this tantalising promise: "You will be like God" (Genesis 3:5).

Since then, the desire to exalt ourselves and diminish God lies behind all sin, and behind all attempts to exert worldly power (which uses strength to subdue, rather than serve, Daniel 11:38). We want to be god of our own lives, and preferably call the shots in other people's as well. And as in Eden, Satan works in and through sinful human power, as he pridefully rages against God's created order. This is serious stuff.

···· 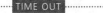 ···
Read John 3:26-31

❓ *How do John's words present a beautiful alternative to exalting self? How will we "become less"?*

Turn these verses into a prayer that exalts Christ and asks for his help to humble yourself.

Raging against God

Having given Daniel a detailed account of a specific period of history to come, the emphasis then shifts. The verses that follow are less tied to specific events, but speak more generally of Christ's enemies throughout time; and those who are "anti Christ" in turn point forward to the Antichrist. Then, in chapter 12, the Lord gives Daniel a glimpse of "the end" of time altogether (Daniel 12:13).

Read Daniel 11:40-45

❓ *Look at the different places mentioned. What do you know about them from elsewhere in the Bible?*

❓ *What is life going to be like for God's people (those in "the Beautiful Land", v 41, 45)?*

This is what lies ahead for Daniel's first readers, and for his readers today: a world dominated by human powers which rage against God and against each other. Sometimes believers are the target; sometimes they're caught in the crossfire. It's chaotic and frightening, but it will "come to [an] end" (v 45).

❓ *Given what is to come, what helpful lessons can readers draw from the previous 10 chapters of Daniel to help them endure it?*

❓ *How might the temptations to compromise be different for us today?*

Bible in a year: Jeremiah 26 – 28 • Ezekiel 13 ⊗

From guilt to grace

The Bible often teaches us about the objective reality of our sin and guilt. This psalm, though, looks at the experience of guilt—at how it feels to be aware of our sin.

David is saying, *If you want to be happy...*

... seek forgiveness

Read Psalm 32:1-5

The psalm begins with a declaration of the goodness, the sweetness, the joy, the "blessedness" of having your sins dealt with.

> ❷ *What images does David use to describe God dealing mercifully with our sins?*
>
> ❷ *What is it like when we ignore our conscience and God's word, and try to carry on with sin (v 3-4)?*
>
> ❷ *Have you ever had this experience?*
>
> ❷ *What is the only thing that can bring relief (v 5)?*

It's interesting that David uses three different words for sin here. David confesses in full, using all the Old Testament words for sin, as he owns his guilt before God.

> ❷ *How does God respond?*

... follow God's ways

Read Psalm 32:6-11

> ❷ *What is the warning to us in verse 6?*

The rising waters call to mind the great flood, that image of God's judgment in Genesis 6 – 9. Just as with the flood, there will come a day when it is too late to turn back to God. We must confess our sins to him now!

The glorious, counter-intuitive truth of the Bible is that safety from God's judgment is not found by running away from him, but in running to him (Psalm 32:7), for he is our Deliverer as well as the Judge.

> ❷ *What makes you sing?*

What makes God sing with happiness? Saving us from our sin (v 7). How wonderful!

In verses 8-9 we hear the voice of the Lord. As he looks back at David's stubborn stupidity in verses 3-4, he warns us that if we refuse to listen to his words of instruction and warning, he will speak to us with physical pain to wake us from our sin.

> ❷ *Verses 10-11 are a joyous conclusion. What is the cause for rejoicing?*

⌄ Apply

Keep short accounts with God. It is a shame that confessing sins in church has gone out of fashion. It makes it that much more important that we make confession part of our regular—daily—spiritual disciplines.

> ❷ *Are you doing this? Will you?*

⌃ Pray

Confess your sins to God now and rejoice in his forgiveness. Try to be as specific as possible. If you can't think of any specific sins to confess, ask the Holy Spirit to prick your conscience. If you still can't think of any, ask your friends, and perhaps start with pride...

Distressing days

This final part of Daniel's vision has in view the "time of the end"—when Christ will return to wrap up human history as we know it and usher in a new creation.

As such, as we read today's verses, we stand much more in Daniel's shoes—not looking back to check the details of history, but looking forward with him in anticipation of God's awesome promises.

Read Daniel 12:1-4

❓ *What great promises are believers given in these verses?*

- *v 1*
- *v 2*
- *v 3*

❓ *What words of warning are there?*

- *v 1*
- *v 2*
- *v 4*

The New Testament adds texture to these promises. Oppression will be a reality for all believers living from Christ's ascension to his return. In Mark 13 Jesus implies that there will be a period when this opposition intensifies, following which "people will see the Son of Man coming in clouds with great power and glory" (Mark 13:26).

When Jesus returns, every person who has ever lived will be raised bodily for eternity; the difference will be in where we'll spend it (see Revelation 20:11-15). Yet for God's people, there is nothing to fear: our names are written in the book of life, and no power of hell or failure on our part can erase it (Daniel 12:1). However it may feel to the contrary, God will deliver us.

The vision is complete (v 4), and Daniel is told to take what he's seen and write it down and roll it up. That is what we have preserved for us in the book of Daniel. While many will look elsewhere to "increase knowledge", it is in the word of God that true wisdom is found.

⌄ Apply

What a promise in verse 3!

❓ *How does this promise for the future encourage you as you seek to "lead [others] to righteousness"? When will you have opportunities to do that this week?*

❓ *Read Philippians 2:14-15. How does this promise for the future challenge you to live distinctively today?*

⌃ Pray

The Lord hath promised good to me,
  His word my hope secures;
He will my shield and portion be
  As long as life endures.

When we've been there ten thousand years,
  Bright shining as the sun,
We've no less days to sing God's praise
  Than when we first begun.

                    Amazing Grace, John Newton

Need to know

"I get that Jesus is going to come back. But, like, when... Why not now?" Someone in today's passage is asking the same question.

When?

Read Daniel 12:5-7

Remember, the man in linen is the Lord Jesus, who Daniel first sees in 10:4-6.

> ❷ *What details in the first half of Daniel 12:7 tell us that the words he's about to speak are important?*
>
> ❷ *What do you make of his answer (v 7)?*

How long until the Lord's return, the end of time, and the final judgment? We can't be sure what the apocalyptic number of "time, times and half a time" means in this context. But we can be sure that "these things will be completed" at a time determined by our sovereign God. Everything we've read in Daniel gives us confidence in that fact.

What?

Read Daniel 12:8-13

> ❷ *How would you paraphrase Daniel's question in verse 8? What kind of attitude does he ask with, do you think?*
>
> ❷ *How do the Lord's words in verses 9-10 reiterate and add to what he said in verses 2-4?*

Verses 11 and 12 use more apocalyptic numbers that are tricky to interpret. Simply put, we don't know how many days are left, but we are to wait patiently, seeking to be faithful until the end (Mark 13:13).

> ❷ *What is Daniel told to do twice (Daniel 12:9, 13)?*
>
> ❷ *What does that mean, do you think?*
>
> ❷ *How is verse 13 a comforting answer to Daniel's question?*

☑ Apply

Daniel humbly asks to know more, and the Lord gently tells him that he knows all that he needs to. As we wait for Jesus' return, there will be unanswered questions. As we search his word and seek to live his way, there will be plenty that we do not fully understand (v 8). But God has revealed everything we need to know to make us wise for salvation (2 Timothy 3:15). So we too must be content to "go our way"—to get on with seeking to be faithful day by day, doing our best with the work he's given us, and trusting that one day he will raise us to new life with him (Daniel 12:13).

> ❷ *"I heard, but I did not understand." As you think back over what you've read in Daniel, and at your life at the moment, is there an area where you feel as Daniel did? What heartfelt questions would you ask the Lord? What would it look like to take verses 9-13 as the answer?*

Read Titus 2:11-14

> ❷ *What should our lives look like as we wait for the appearing of Jesus Christ?*

Ask him to help you live like that by his Spirit.

The beginning of the end

The big message that we've seen time and again in Daniel is that God rules. So what are the implications of that for us today?

If you were looking to find a New Testament counterpart to the book of Daniel, it would probably have to be 1 Peter. Peter wrote "to God's elect, exiles, scattered throughout" Asia Minor (modern-day Turkey) (1 Peter 1:1). Peter's point is that all believers are exiles in a foreign land—living on earth but longing to go home, to heaven. While we wait, we live among a people who do not know our God. Daniel is a book which teaches us how to do that well. Here are four big take-homes to finish our series with.

Do good for God's glory
Read 1 Peter 2:11-12

❓ *When in Daniel have we...*
- *seen believers keep themselves from sin?*
- *witnessed believers live good lives that caused pagans to give glory to God?*
- *been encouraged to have our eyes fixed "on the day [God] visit us" (i.e. Jesus' return)?*

Submit to authority
Read 1 Peter 2:13-17

❓ *When in Daniel have we...*
- *watched believers submit to earthly authority and honour the king?*
- *been reminded that all authority is "sent by" God?*
- *seen believers "fear God" and live as his "slaves", first and foremost?*

Humble yourself
Read 1 Peter 5:5-7

❓ *When in Daniel have we...*
- *seen that "God opposes the proud but shows favour to the humble" (v 5)?*
- *been called to humble ourselves before God, so that we will be lifted up (v 6)?*
- *been encouraged to ask for God's help in prayer (v 7)?*

Endure suffering
Read 1 Peter 4:12-13; 5:8-11

❓ *When in Daniel have we...*
- *witnessed believers be tested by suffering (4:12)?*
- *been warned that "the family of believers" should expect opposition (5:9)?*
- *been encouraged that God will one day ultimately restore us, and will help us to stand firm until then (v 10)?*
- *seen that power belongs to God for ever and ever (v 11)?*

⌃ Pray

Which of those principles do you most need God's help to live out? Ask him to help you to remember the lessons of Daniel, and to live out your years in exile faithfully, as he did.

JUDE: Contend

Jude is the fifth-shortest book of the Bible—but it is also one of the hardest-hitting. It's as if the author is writing in CAPITALS throughout. Buckle up...

Since it's a short letter, today we'll look over the whole of it, before going into greater depth over the following four days.

Read Jude 1-25

From and to

❓ *How does the writer describe himself (v 1)?*

"Jude" and "Judas" are the same name. And the only James in the New Testament who had a brother called Jude/Judas is the James who had a mother called Mary, a father called Joseph... and a half-brother called Jesus (Matthew 13:55). So we're likely reading the words of someone who knew Jesus very, very well—and yet who is humble enough not to trumpet that, but to call himself a "servant of Jesus Christ" (Jude v 1).

❓ *How does Jude describe the Christians to whom he's writing (v 1, 3)?*

The problem

Read Jude 4, 8, 16-19

❓ *How would you sum up what Jude wants to warn his Christian friends about?*

❓ *Why does he think it matters so much?*

❓ *What should the readers of this letter do?*
- *v 3*
- *v 20-21*
- *v 22-23*

The promise

❓ *What can they know that God is able to do, even as they face the dangers outlined in this letter (v 24)?*

❓ *Imagine receiving this letter. How might you feel by the end of...*
- *v 2?*
- *v 16?*
- *v 23?*
- *v 25?*

❓ *(Without looking further down the page) If you had to sum up the message of the letter as a whole in one sentence, what would you say?*

Here's my attempt to sum up the theme of Jude: *those whom God keeps, must keep the faith.*

🔼 Pray

Pray that God would use this letter to change and challenge you, and that your heart would be ready to respond in faith to what the Holy Spirit shows you.

Then use the words of verses 24-25 to praise God for who he is, and what he is able to do for his faithful people.

A serious warning

Jude had wanted to write to these Christian friends about something, but then found that he had to write to them a very different kind of letter.

Slipped in secretly

Read Jude 1-4

- ❷ *What had he wanted to write to them about (v 3)?*
- ❷ *What did he feel "compelled" to write to them about instead (v 3)?*
- ❷ *Why (v 4)?*

Keeping the faith means holding to the "once for all" truths that the Bible teaches and God's people have always held to. It is not our truth—it is God's, and it has been "entrusted" to us to handle with humility and care. Keeping the faith requires effort—we are to "contend", not just sit back. And it is the responsibility of all Jude's readers—which ultimately means every Christian, including you.

And it is necessary—because in the church today, just as in Jude's time, "ungodly people" teach dangerous error. And they do it "secretly". False teachers don't come with a flashing "Warning" sign or a siren.

So, how can they be recognised? Verse 4 explains: they teach that because Jesus is full of grace, the clear moral teaching of the Bible need not apply in our context or our culture. They deny that Jesus is the only God or that Jesus is our supreme authority.

···· TIME OUT ·······································

- ❷ *Have you seen immorality or a denial of Jesus' lordship taught or promoted within churches?*

- ❷ *How was it dealt with (if at all)?*
- ❷ *How does that compare to what Jude says in these verses?*

Heading for disaster

Read Jude 5-7

- ❷ *What three "case studies" does Jude list out here? (If you have time, reading Numbers 13:1 – 14:45; Genesis 6:1-3 and Genesis 13:12-13; 19:1-29 will help you.)*
- ❷ *What point do you think Jude is trying to make, repeat and underline?*

The truth is that there were people who left Egypt, who counted themselves among Gods' people, but were not allowed into the promised land. There were angels who were banished from God's throneroom and consigned to outer darkness (2 Peter 2:4). There are those who "suffer the punishment of eternal fire" instead of enjoying eternity with Christ (Jude v 7). God's judgment is real, it is terrible, and no one is beyond it. And it is where false teaching leads, because it draws people away from trusting in Christ to save them and give them eternal life in glory. False teaching may come with a smile, but it is a smile that beckons people to hell.

❯ Apply

- ❷ *Is there someone you need to warn about listening to false teaching today?*

The easy way to hell

You might think the examples and warnings in verses 5-7 are enough. Jude doesn't. He has four more brief examples to give us. Why? Because this matters eternally.

Denying God's authority

Read Jude 8-10

The story in verse 9 comes from outside the Old Testament. But this shouldn't trouble us: Jude is writing under the inspiration of the Holy Spirit. What Jude tells us about this event really happened. The point? Even great archangels cannot presume to place themselves in God's judgment seat but remain under God's authority: yet these false teachers "reject [God's] authority" (v 8).

God's authority is rejected when we call wrong what he does not, *and* when we fail to call wrong what he calls wrong. It is not our place to condemn anyone, but it *is* our place to call out as wrong all that God forbids—no more, but also no less. Love does not affirm people in their sin all the way to eternal punishment, nor tolerate those who beckon believers to follow them there (v 10).

Deadly popular

Read Jude 11-13

Jude is not holding back. The "way of Cain" is to be driven by envy, and to ignore God's warnings (Genesis 4:1-16). "Balaam's error" is to preach what makes money and pleases the world, not what God has revealed (Numbers 22 – 24; 31:16; Joshua 13:22). "Korah's rebellion" is to seek to replace the authority of God's chosen leader of his people with your own (Numbers 16:1-35). And this is the path that the false teachers in Jude's day have chosen—though, of course, they have not realised that and would never describe it like that.

> ❷ *Given all this, why are the images Jude uses in Jude 12-13 appropriate?*

Read Jude 14-16

In verses 14-15 the Spirit again inspires Jude to reach outside Scripture—this time, to the First Book of Enoch. God is coming in judgment—and "defiant words ... spoken against him" (v 15) bring conviction.

Grumbling and fault-finding in verse 16 probably means grumbling against God and fault-finding with God. Jude constantly refers to Old Testament events, so here he is likely referring to Israel's grumbling about God in the wilderness (Exodus 16).

Imagine these false teachers. They're wealthy, encourage people to reinterpret challenging parts of Scripture, and reshape their view of God to suit their own desires. It's not hard to imagine why they might be popular.

> ❷ *What further reason for their popularity does Jude give (end of Jude 16)?*

⌃ Pray

Pray for your church leaders, that they would teach and contend for the truth. And pray that when the time comes (and it will) you would stand clearly and firmly against dangerous false teaching, too.

Four defences

The road to hell is paved with fine-sounding, friendly false teaching. How should Christians respond? Jude calls us to do four things…

Number one

Read Jude 17-19

❓ *Why should we not be surprised by the presence of false teaching within churches (v 17-18)?*

A great danger when it comes to false teaching is that, deep down, we refuse to believe it could happen in our churches. This is not to say we all need to turn into heresy-hunters, flinging accusations and leaving churches if we disagree over a secondary issue such as Sabbath rest, drinking alcohol, church government, etc. But it *is* to say that we must guard against an attitude of "It will never happen in this church" or "I know that's wrong, but I don't want to cause offence by opposing it" or "I know that's dangerous teaching—I hope someone will say something to him/her about it".

No—Jesus' apostles said those who scoff (perhaps very politely and eloquently) at Jesus' teaching would come. We should expect them to be proved right.

Numbers two and three

Read Jude 20-21

❓ *In what two ways can we "keep [ourselves] in God's love" (v 21)?*

If we don't know what God has said, we will not be able to contend for it. The better we know the truth, the quicker we'll spot the lie. The more we've thought about how the

Bible applies to controversial issues such as sexual morality, race, transgender issues, and so on, the better we'll be at noticing when someone slips in some error.

❓ *What are you doing to make sure you know the word as deeply as possible?*

But we can't do it by our own efforts or intelligence. Eternal dangers require divine help to avoid—so we must be praying, too (v 20). The Spirit, who dwells in us, enables us to pray to God as our Father (Romans 8:15)—and so when we pray, we rely on the Spirit.

❓ *How are you ensuring that you pray about what you read in the word or hear from the pulpit?*

Number four

Re-read Jude 20-21

❓ *What are we waiting for (v 21)?*
❓ *How does this make all the effort of contending for the faith worthwhile?*

Christians are a waiting people. We know our best days lie ahead of us, and that they will arrive when the Lord Jesus, in his mercy, returns to save and to judge.

⌃ Pray

❓ *How have these verses encouraged you? Challenged you?*

Speak to God about your answers now.

He is able

Those whom God keeps, keep the faith—and they encourage, urge and beg others to as well. The obedience of other church members to our Lord must be <u>your</u> concern.

You must help

Read Jude 22-23

With wonderful wisdom, Jude identifies three types of struggling Christian. For each, loving them well will look different.

> ❷ *To those who are starting to listen to false teaching and doubt what God's word says, how should we respond (v 22)?*

Don't leave someone in their doubts, but don't jump all over them. They need the mercy of being listened to, of being kindly spoken to, and of being loved throughout.

> ❷ *For those who have gone further, starting to disagree with the truth, what should we do (v 23a)?*

If someone walks past a burning building, they should both warn people not to enter and seek to drag people out. When we risk causing offence or being rejected in order to call a brother or sister out of an error that leads to the "fire" of judgment, this is what we are doing.

> ❷ *For those who have actively disobeyed the truth (perhaps in sexual immorality, v 4), what should we do (v 23b)?*

Be careful, says Jude. As we hold out mercy to those who have fallen for the lie that sin is not sin, or is not serious, we must take care not to fall into the same trap. We must not give up on a fallen brother or sister— but nor can we allow them to continue wearing the "clothes" of immorality. We need to tell them to "get changed"—to repent and seek God's forgiveness—so they can enjoy fellowship with Jesus once again.

⌄ Apply

> ❷ *Do you know anyone who is in any one of these three struggling "categories"?*

> ❷ *They need your help. What will you do to help them today?*

You need help

Jude has called us to a difficult life—the life of contending for the gospel, otherwise known as the Christian life. We need help!

Read Jude 24-25

> ❷ *What is God able to do (v 24)?*

Look back over your Christian life, with its spiritual ups and downs. Every day, God was keeping you. Every time you tripped, he caught you before you stumbled. You can rely on him—our glorious, majestic, powerful and authoritative Lord and Saviour. Those whom God keeps, keep the faith.

⌄ Apply

Think back over the letter as a whole.

> ❷ *How has it changed your view of...*
> * *false teaching?*
> * *the Christian life?*
> * *God's love for us?*

Brave by Faith

God-Sized Confidence in a Post-Christian World

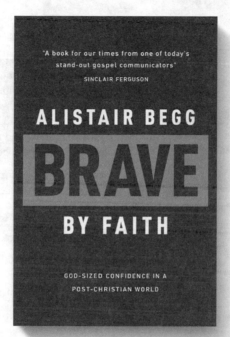

In this realistic, positive book, renowned Bible teacher Alistair
Begg examines the first seven chapters of Daniel to show us
that living by faith in Daniel's God will enable us to live bravely,
confidently and obediently in an increasingly secular society.

thegoodbook.co.uk/brave
thegoodbook.com/brave
thegoodbook.com.au/brave

Introduce a friend to

explore

If you're enjoying using *Explore*, why not introduce a friend? Time with God is our introduction to daily Bible reading and is a great way to get started with a regular time with God. It includes 28 daily readings along with articles, advice and practical tips on how to apply what the passage teaches.

Why not order a copy for someone you would like to encourage?

Coming up next...

- **Romans**
  with Timothy Keller

- **Joel**
  with Jonathan Griffiths

- **Jeremiah**
  with Dave Griffith-Jones

- **Colossians**
  with Mark Meynell